They're All Trying To Kill Me!

(Or How I Manage To Survive As A Flight Instructor)

By

Jeremy Vandersluis

ISBN: 1-4033-5423-5 (e-book)
ISBN: 1-4033-5424-3 (Paperback)

Library of Congress Control Number: 2002093281

This book is printed on acid free paper.

Printed in the United States of America
Bloomington, IN

1st Books - rev. 09/06/02

Contents

Introduction

"They are all trying to kill me!" - That is how I answered my boss when he asked me for my feelings at the end of my first week as a flight instructor. I said it with feeling having just come back from another brush with death, loosely describable as a flying lesson. Soon after, my boss, mentor and friend, Rex Gasteiger, started suggesting that I keep a record of some of my experiences for the purposes of 'entertaining a wider audience.' I maintain that he was actually expecting one of those students to get me, and wanted a record of my last days on the planet as a warning to new and up-and-coming CFI's (Certified Flight Instructor.) Anyway, Rex kept bugging me and here are the results...

I have tried to keep accounts of these incidents as factual as possible... Any humor is purely in the mind of the reader... A lot of these 'events' were damn scary at the time! There are a few tips for the budding pilot. There are a lot of things in aviation that you just pick up along the way and that are never actually taught. I hope I can reveal a few of them. This isn't a 'How-to' or a piloting manual, but there are some tricks that have been useful to me and I share them, at no extra charge, in the hope that someone out there avoids a screw-up which may have been averted.

As an instructor I have been described as great, fabulous, wonderful and given other high accolades, but these were mainly by myself... I have also been described as tyrannical, bullying and intimidating, but that was mainly by my girlfriend who was one of my students at the time. I can't be that bad because she later became my wife.

There are several categories here; stuff that happened during my pilot training, stuff that happened since I qualified as a fully fledged pilot, stuff that has happened to me as an instructor and stuff that has happened to other friends and colleagues that I have been able to substantiate. I have left out the hangar flyer's best friends, folklore, myth and urban legend. For this and other gossip, visit your local airport. I don't know why airports are so rife with gossip, but they are and it can be great fun. Maybe in the next book.

Thanks go to Ute, Rex, Claude, Keri, Jim, Jonty, Markus, Pete, Tim, Dick, Ross, Joëlle, Frank at the Airport Pilot Shop and many of my students without whom this book would not have been possible. I don't know why am I thanking these people? If I hadn't written this book I'd have gotten a lot more sleep!

I have used additional material from, and with the kind permission of, the following people:

Rob Mixon
Jim Leon
Noeru Kubo
Don Lindsay
Jeff Van West

A Budding Pilot - Flying starts with watching the sky and dreaming.

It All Begins...

I must have been about ten or eleven years old when I first got the chance to go up in an aircraft. My youngest sister had been invited to go up with her best friend, whose father, Ross, had a share in a small Piper. I looked so miserable that not inviting me would have been inhumane. Being born and growing up in Windsor, I was under the flight path of, and only ten miles from Heathrow. Looking up at the sky whenever a plane went by was something that I just always did. If you asked me what I wanted to be when I was a kid, the answer was probably slightly unusual, either a computer programmer or a singer. It was the other kids that said fireman, astronaut or pilot. But, I believe that everybody has a secret wish to fly, a belief which has been strengthened by my instructing experiences. The first flight with Ross was relatively tame and over quickly as my sister wasn't enjoying it. We landed, dropped off the girls, stopped for orange juice and biscuits and taxied back out. Just Ross and me this time. Ross took us to a safe altitude and let me take the controls. I remember asking him to take the controls back saying that I didn't like it and that it was too much power. Easy to remember as that was the only time in my piloting career that I have said 'too much power.' Now there is a constant mantra of 'got to get more power...' Soon after Ross took the controls again, I quite suddenly felt ill. Sickness was not something we had talked about before the flight so I did not know where to look for a sick-sack. Clamping my hand over my mouth was not the best solution to the problem. Have you ever pressed your thumb over the business end of a tap? It sprays everywhere, doesn't it? The mixture of biscuits and orange juice is also not ideal if you are planning on taking kids aloft. On contact with a warm cockpit, it forms something akin to quick drying cement. I spoke to Ross a couple of years ago, some twenty years after the event. He and his fellow share owners were still finding and chipping off orange concrete even then. An auspicious start to a wonderful career in aviation!

Shaky Start...

A trial flight is how many people start flying or get hooked on aviation. Trial by flight would be a better description in my case. I fly more in spite of that particular joy ride rather than because of it. I went along to my local airfield and went for a half-hour ride. Even though the turbulence was not heavy, I had to ask for the flight to be cut short as I was soon feeling ill. I had always been a very bad passenger on boats and not even a very good passenger in cars. I was worried that I would never be able to get over my motion sickness and that my passion for flying would have to go unrequited. It took me a while but now I like a rough ride!

Takeoff!

I found myself living and working in the very beautiful town of Namur in Belgium. The office canteen served excellent meals but I started losing weight after just two days. I was mesmerized as I watched planes takeoff and land on Namur Aerodrome's grass strip, just outside the canteen window. Every lunchtime I left the office and spent my lunch hour at the aerodrome. I spoke to an instructor in my broken French, inquiring what I would have to do to get my license. He wasn't too interested by me. Probably due to my unimpressive French and the fact that my hair was long in those days, very long. I certainly didn't fit the Top-Gun profile. In Belgium, even before you can be a student pilot, you must 'survive' at least a private pilots medical certificate and receive your student pilots license. The system in Belgium is, or used to be, slow. It took me a month to complete the 5 different visits required for obtention of the medical and then another three weeks waiting for the license and logbook. The system is designed to dissuade people from learning to fly and a senior administrator in the Belgian flight authority is on record as having said that, "Aviation [in Belgium] would be fine if it wasn't for all the pilots." The instructor was therefore surprised to see me, a couple of months later, waving my student pilot's certificate and shaven-headed. I have always been prone to radical appearance swings! A first lesson was booked. Just like my trial flight, I had to cut it short because I was feeling queasy. I was angry and frustrated with myself, but I flatly refused to let feeling ill get in the way of me going up in the air. Every lesson I felt a little better and now I feel I have beaten the illness. Part of not feeling ill was understanding what motion sickness is. Get to know the enemy! Even now, I do occasionally feel a little bit 'off-color,' on a hot bumpy day as a passenger, but I know how to deal with it and can 'think' my way out of it.

Student Pilot - Why wait for someone else to kill you when you can do a perfectly good job all on your own.

First Steps...

On the way to becoming a safe pilot, the grail for all pilots, everybody goes through a phase where the elation and euphoria of flight totally masks good judgment. The instructor says, "Okay, you're on your own," and instead of saying, "What! Are you totally nuts?" and shutting down the engine, we go it alone... First solo. It is however an event to be remembered for the remainder of ones life... however short one cares to make it! The early solo flights are usually just circuits of the airport, a standard traffic pattern. I say 'usually,' because my own instructor has told me of some notable variations and I had a few unusual solo flights myself.

Do You Remember The First Time?

Most pilots can give fairly accurate accounts of their first solo flight. The details of my own first solo are fairly uninteresting, the whole thing passed off very smoothly. It isn't the technical aspect which I remember, rather the feelings, the emotions and the loudness (but not of the engine.) All the way along the downwind leg of my circuit, with a short pause for a radio call, I shouted "Yeahhhhhh…" as loud as my lungs would allow. I don't often shout in the air anymore. The rules about aircraft noise are becoming stricter and stricter! Besides, my students complain that it deafens them over the intercom.

Anyone For Seconds? A Close Call…

My second solo flight was an event that I still remember vividly. Not so much for the flight itself, but certainly for the way it ended, and the reaction of my first instructor, Claude Cheilletz. It started out just fine. A perfect circuit on the uncontrolled, 1,800ft grass runway 06 at Namur, Belgium (EBNM.) As I went around my circuit I made my normal radio calls and heard an incoming pilot request landing information. He was told the runway in use and announced his intention to join the circuit. A minute or two passed. I called downwind and was echoed just seconds later by his downwind call. I remember looking anxiously behind me to see how close he was. When I turned base, a minute later, he again echoed my call this time almost immediately. Another flurry of head turning, neck craning and eye straining produced no results. I called final and got set up for the landing. When after a few moments I heard the call from the 'enemy pilot,' I again had a good look round to no avail. I had studied hard… I knew that the rules of the air give right of way to the lower aircraft and I was sure there was nobody lower than I. Just 20 feet above the grass, I saw another plane on the other end of the runway coming straight for me. I immediately turned to the right, started to go around, keyed the mike and 'expressed myself.' * Later the operator of Namur Radio, the lovely Lucia, remarked on how good my French had become, and how much emotion I had managed to inject into just a few short expletives. When I got on the ground and back into the office, the pilot of the other plane, also a C150, with the tail number OO-PRL, was being held against a wall by his lapels with just the tips of his feet touching the ground. Claude, my instructor, was explaining what runway 06 meant, and how it would be an awfully good idea if the guy learned to point his plane in the same direction he said he was going to point it in. Claude was also 'expressing himself,' * and with even greater imagination than I had managed.

* The actual language we used whilst 'expressing ourselves,' has been deleted to make this text publishable. It is also possible that some of our suggestions to the mystery pilot (name withheld) involved acts which are illegal in most countries and would involve greater than average flexibility.

More Seconds? Nights Under The Fan...

With me it must be something about second solo flights because when, fairly recently, I did my second night solo on the way to a commercial rotorcraft-helicopter add-on rating, I had problems again. After a number of good circuits, the tower instructed me to leave the pattern to the North and hold two miles away from the airport while they waited for the arrival of a plane with a total electrical failure. No radio and no external lighting at all. I felt bad for the pilot of the fixed wing aircraft. The guy got safely to the ground and taxied clear without incident, I am pleased to say. Soon after, I was called back into the circuit. My instructor, Joe, had not been listening to the radio but had been watching me. He was more than a little nervous to see me leave the pattern on my own at night. It is very easy to get lost in the dark, even if the airport is lit up like a Christmas tree.

Lost But Not Forgotten...

One major point, and actually quite important milestone, in learning to be a pilot is getting lost. Getting lost in the car is nothing by comparison. In the car you pull over, ask someone for directions, look at the map, road signs, whatever... If you run out of gas... no big deal. In an aircraft, landing to ask the way at a corner shop is frowned upon. It is very difficult to see the road signs from 3,000 feet, and the maps we use have a strange way of bearing no resemblance whatsoever to the ground we are flying over. Running out of gas can ruin your whole day, not to mention the fact that the nice people at the Federal Aviation Authority (FAA) will ask some awkward questions and may want to borrow your license for a while! I maintain that if you are going to get lost, you may as well do it in style. It was my first real solo cross country flight. From my home aerodrome of Namur in Belgium, to Kortrijk, then St. Ghislain and back to Namur. All went well until St.

Ghislain, but then on the way home I missed a couple of checkpoints... The first thing that gave me a clue that I may be some distance off course was watching a 737 pass some 500 feet over my head. I immediately realized that I must be in the busy Class Charlie airspace around Charleroi airport. That made it easy to find my way home. I called Charleroi tower (Brussels South) and confessed my wrong doing. They were very friendly and helpful, giving me a vector to get me home, and limiting their complaints to suggesting that according to local custom, contact should be made with approach or the tower before entering the zone. When I arrived back at Namur, Claude was not quite as friendly. He had already answered two phone calls from Charleroi tower. They had told him it might be nice to explain to me that same local custom.

Why's It Gone So Quiet...

When out on a cross country with Claude one day, we received a clearance into, and vectors through, the Liege TMA. The controllers had given us something of a game until that point and the routing they had given us was not our greatest source of pleasure. After receiving our latest vector, everything went quiet for some 8 or 10 minutes. It probably should have struck us as strange that in the busy airspace around Liege, nobody was talking, but Claude was busy teaching me and I was busy flying so neither of us picked it up. Sometime later, Claude started grumbling that the controllers were not doing their jobs properly and that we should have been given another vector by now. He may also have suggested that the standard of service "was fairly typical from the incompetent idiots working this sector." I noticed something unusual and asked Claude why the little light on the radio was remaining on. Claude went very pale. Throughout our entire transition of the airspace, his mike switch had been stuck down. Every word had been heard by the "incompetent idiots." He fixed his mike switch, called approach control and requested a new vector (which we were given immediately.) Approach control mentioned very matter-of-factly that we should be careful to ensure that our microphone switch did not get stuck in this sector ever again, but there was a fairly clear implication that we should not even bother bringing our microphone switch into the sector ever again. Strangely, after that Claude and I said almost nothing to each other until we had landed the airplane.

Jeremy D. I. Vandersluis

Instruments Of Torture...

Smoke, fog and family is a reasonable summary of my first real ILS approach in instrument flight conditions... Just a week or two after gaining my instrument rating I was already well into preparing myself for my commercial pilot certificate. One of the requirements was a long cross country flight. My brother, who was then working on his private license, was visiting me at the time and was along for the ride. The trip was full of 'new experiences.' Before we could start out, I had to get checked out on a Cessna 182, a flight which was in itself eventful. The ceiling was low, about 800 feet. The rain started as we took off and lightning flickered during the whole checkout, but nevertheless the checkout was completed and we managed to get on the ground safely. Another necessity before leaving for the flight, which we had chosen to make at night, was that I become night current, allowing the carriage of passengers, by making a few landings to a full stop in night conditions. All went well. To set the scene then, new type of airplane, new to unsupervised night flight and newly qualified as an instrument pilot, we picked up a favorable forecast and set off from Naples around midnight. At the first stop, Orlando, I noticed that the plane was only

12

drawing fuel from the right tank! A little scary since I was unable to find any maintenance staff to help with the problem. After refueling we continued on to Jacksonville arriving in the general area to find forest fire smoke so thick, even at 7,000 feet, that visibility was basically zero. Descending brought escape from smoke and entry into cloud. Following vectors from approach, I centered my needles, just as I had been trained, and kept up my concentration as I slid down the ILS glide path. As I prepared to call the missed approach, just ten feet above the decision height, I popped out of cloud and there it was! What a beautiful sight. I actually got a lump in my throat and the tear in my eye wasn't totally from the smoke. All I had learned really worked! The tower called me before I was clear of the runway to ask the altitude at which I had 'broken out.' I was apparently the first successful approach after seven larger aircraft, all jets, had 'gone missed.' The field was covered in patchy fog and we taxied in slowly. We parked in front of the FBO and quickly installed ourselves in the pilots lounge. A couple of hours sleep later I awoke looking up at the sky! We found out that about three hours before our arrival, a tornado had ripped a corner of the roof off, some sliding, corrugated steel hangar doors were bent over like sheets of paper and the ramp area in which we had parked our trusty C182 had been a direct hit. The view across the ramp was saddening. Several aircraft, although properly secured at the time, were badly damaged. I saw the owner of a single engine Cessna walk around his airplane in total disbelief. The wingtips were still tied down but the airplane was on its back. Another aircraft owner was crying. His light twin (I think it was a Cessna 414) had another aircraft twisted around it!

Oh Brother...

My brother was involved in another scare. While visiting me in Florida, and prior to me receiving my instructor's ticket, he flew with one of the most senior instructors on the field. A cross country flight. The weather was far short of perfect. When my brother and his instructor had not returned at the appropriate time, I became more and more concerned. When, 45 minutes later, a call was received from the Flight Service Station (FSS), inquiring as to their safe arrival, I almost went mad with worry. The weather had now deteriorated to the normal South Florida afternoon storm state that makes it impossible to see more than a few hundred feet, and they were out there in a Cessna 152! Or so I thought. In they walked, all smiles, minutes after the rain stopped. They had been sitting outside in the C152 for an hour, to avoid the rain. They had forgotten to close their flight plan. Not the kind of error that one expects from someone with a 'Master CFI' designation, but we instructors are human too!

Getting Geared Up...

Just before taking my commercial instrument ticket I had to go out and get some experience in a complex airplane. Tim was on his first day at the flight school and was assigned to check me out on the Piper Comanche. I didn't like Tim when I first met him and it took me some time to warm to him. Now I think he's great, but a close call will always bring you closer to the one you share it with! What I didn't doubt was that he was a good and capable instructor and that he knew the Comanche. As a student pilot at any level, even for advanced ratings, you just don't think of questioning your instructor's qualifications. We had been flying for about two and a half hours in the pattern, just doing circuits, getting used to cycling the gear. Suddenly Tim and I exchanged worried glances. I had moved the gear selector to the gear down position and we had both seen the manual (emergency) gear extension lever moving on its own. We talked about it. The gear light was glowing green confirming that the gear was down and locked, but there was no doubt about it, the manual gear extension lever had moved on its own. We decided to leave the gear down rather than attempting to cycle it just in case the next time it did not lock. We also decided to tell the tower what had happened and make a pass over the tower to have them check that the gear was down. They said it all looked good and we decided to go around the pattern one last time and come in for a landing. As we turned from base leg to final approach, the school's chief pilot and charter pilot came on the radio and told us, everybody else on the frequency, the tower and the tape recorder in the tower that the manual gear extension lever in the Comanche was supposed to move as the gear extended, in fact it moves every time the gear is extended or retracted. We landed and taxied in silence. I wanted to be angry with Tim, but since I had not noticed a metal lever almost two feet long moving from the horizontal to the vertical, probably twenty times during the course of a two and a half hour flight, I had to see the funny side. We talked about it later and agreed that neither of us had seen the lever move until that one moment when we both got that hot prickly feeling in the smalls of our backs. Anyway, I ended up with the requisite number of hours in the Comanche, and so did Tim! Observational skills are directly affected by workload, if you are too busy, you are not going to notice the Jumbo Jet coming straight for you. Pilots train until flying is second nature in order to give themselves a better chance of noticing and handling the unexpected. Once you reach a certain level of experience, it is fairly unusual to miss stuff like an engine falling off the wing or the window at the front having a better than normal view of the ground.

Backing Out...

I noticed early on that the small training aircraft we use have no reverse gear. Most of the heavy jet aircraft flying around have the capability of reversing their thrust and could, if they had to, push themselves backwards... But they don't, they wait for the aircraft tug (which uses a lot less fuel and makes a lot less noise.) Pulling light aircraft backwards, by hand, without help is an unwelcome chore which surprises all new pilots. Belgium, or more particularly Namur was a great place to learn to fly. Apart from learning how to drag planes around, I was exposed to a number of special circumstances that we have to simulate here in Florida. On an 1,800 foot strip every takeoff or landing is an exercise in short-field technique. On a grass surface, crosswind technique is especially important. Because of the reduced traction/friction with the surface it is easy to slide around. When the ground gets wet at Namur, puddles form on the surface sufficient for water skiers to get a workout. In aviation terms, there is significant risk of aquaplaning. If the rain continues for any length of time, and take it from me, in Belgium it does, the ground becomes soft and boggy to the extent that wooly mammoths could sink without a trace. After a particularly damp autumn, there were a number of areas near, and even on the runway, which were marked out, with traffic cones, as "soft and non-navigable." I taxied out for some solo circuits avoiding the worst spots. I lined up on the runway and checked my gyro alignment against the compass. I can't have been stationary for more than four or five seconds, and then I went to full power. The airplane rolled forward just a couple of feet in a very sluggish and unsatisfying fashion. After a couple of feet more, the nose-wheel became completely stuck and began sinking in some fresh mud. I managed to pull the power and stop the prop before I had sunk in to the ground enough for it to make contact. It is bad enough sitting in the cockpit waiting to be rescued... But it is even worse being pulled out of the marshes, tail-first, by a tractor. I visited the aerodrome bar with the intention of regaining my pride and morale. As I walked through the door, almost everybody stood and applauded, a couple of people mimed me coming to an abrupt halt whilst a couple of others mimed me being towed all the way to the ramp, backwards! My soft-field technique is better now, but just-in-case the conditions are bad there, next time I visit, I am planning on getting a seaplane rating.

Are You Ready For This?

Many flight schools require candidates to go through a mock checkride with a senior instructor or an instructor other than their own before being allowed to take the checkride with the examiner. My pre-check was with the wife of the school owner, Nikki. I had known her a couple of months, but never flown with her. I have no idea why she made me so nervous… She just did! We did a short oral test and I convinced her that I knew which end of the plane to point down the runway. My pseudo examiner was about 5ft 2in tall and used a couple of cushions to reach the rudder pedals and see over the glare shield. We preflighted together and apart from having a few problems adjusting Nikki's seat to the full forward position, all looked good. As I took off and started initial climb, Nikki just disappeared! Her seat, whose locking pin had been broken in the attempt to move it all the way to the front, slid backwards at such a speed that it broke free of one of the rails on which it traveled, making it impossible to move it again in flight. To Nikki's credit, she did not grab at the yoke as she slid backwards. We elected to continue the flight, but whenever Nikki wanted to demonstrate something to me, I had to handle the rudder! The check went pretty well and I was satisfied with my performance though I remained nervous throughout. My final trial was to be a short field landing over not the traditional 50ft threshold object, but a 100ft object just to prove I was truly ready! I set everything up perfectly, cleared my imaginary threshold obstruction by inches and started to reduce speed. Had I been flying a helicopter, I would have entered the hover about 4 feet above the ground, unfortunately I was flying a Cessna 172 with very poor hover characteristics. I bled the airspeed off the bottom of the scale keeping the plane flying with full flap, almost full power with the nose as high as I could pull it and a large amount of will power. The plane fell the last 4 feet almost vertically, bounced once, again almost vertically, and stopped with a ground roll of about 20 feet! I would be surprised if we used more than 400ft of runway in total. It is a good thing Nikki, who burst out laughing, had her cushion! I started pleading my case immediately, saying that it was nerves, that I had never done that before and my instructor would confirm that all my landings were perfect or near perfect. At that moment, the tower called, "**Harrier** 950AC, Naples, Taxi up to the first exit and in to the ramp on this frequency." Nikki was still laughing when she got out. I was still blushing!

Tradition...

Different schools have different ways of celebrating milestones in students' aviation career progression. Many cut off ties or shirt tails and write something commemorative on them, many have dousings with water (baptisms), some just certificates and others much more elaborate rituals. For my private license in Belgium, I got a bucket of water. For my commercial certificate in the USA, I got hit with not one, but THREE large trash cans of water. I was so totally soaked that I went straight out to the parking lot, stripped off all my clothes except for a wet T-shirt and put on some swimming trunks I was going to use on the beach later in the day. I then went back out to the flight line where I had my photo taken on the wing of the Comanche I had flown during the checkride. I was unaware of the stir that I was causing walking through the FBO in just beachwear. There are people at the airport, some of whom I don't even know, that recognize me as 'That Speedo guy.' People who don't know my face still know who I am if I introduce myself as the Speedo guy.

Other Traditions…

There are, of course, other rites of passage and initiations to help advancing pilots celebrate their accomplishments. One of my favorites is 'The G Test.' The newly certified pilot is told that, as a qualified pilot, they are going to have to be able to take a certain G Force. The way to test their aptitude is then explained. In addition to the pilot, you need five strong men and a solid, four legged table, the kind that you find in a modern classroom or library with a metal frame and a plastic covered wooden top is best. The table is turned on its back and the pilot lays down inside it. Four of the men take a table leg each, and one of the pilot's arms or legs to secure them. Rope or belts can be used to make the whole thing safer. The extra man tells them to lift, gives a countdown, and conducts the swinging. When the amplitude of the swing is taking the table to the vertical with the pilot feet first, instead of going over the top as the stooge/pilot expects, the table is brought to an abrupt halt with the victim being suspended by his legs (that's why you need strong men for this one!) The fifth member of the squad runs off to get the funnel and bucket of water or water hose that has been hidden nearby, and the hapless hero gets it

23

down the trouser leg! We actually managed to get the same guy twice by promising to go over the top for real on his next checkride… Sucker!

Qualified Pilot Or 'Licensed To Kill' - The Pilot Is The One At The Front Who Knows What He Is Doing, Right?

Which Way Is Up?

When I started flying, I had a few problems with motion sickness. Whilst I no longer have these problems, I have revisited those feelings in 'extreme circumstances.' Guy Bruyninx is a retired airline pilot, aerobatic and display pilot extraordinaire, septuagenarian and a damn nice chap. The first time out with Guy was fun. Actually that doesn't begin to describe it. It was stupendous! We went out to an area reserved for aerobatics, he demonstrated each maneuver and then let me loose to try it. What a blast! Second time out he tried to kill me! He said to me he would show me a simple display routine that he was working on. After the first flight, I knew what I was in for so I felt relaxed, certainly exhilarated, but relaxed. Then, all of a sudden, my world folded in on itself. The sky wasn't where I had left it just a moment before. The ground was not doing what the ground is supposed to do. The plane, a Robin D2160, OO-VLU, wasn't flying, it was tumbling backwards, end over end. My stomach on the other hand was tumbling forwards, end over end. Relief washed over me as we returned to level flight, albeit inverted. We picked up speed and entered a tight outside loop from the bottom. I think that was my introduction to the comforts of negative G's, about 3 of them. Just one of those had me gibbering. When Guy rolled back to the normal, sunny side up position, I breathed another sigh of relief. Very short lived! Guy pushed the stick over to enter another outside loop, this time entering from the top to complete his vertical '8.' Alright, everyone has their limit. Mine was something that was so far behind me as to be only a distant memory. I skipped over the asking and pleading parts and went straight to some of the more advanced groveling techniques, "Please stop. Please! Please take me home! I want to get off now. I feel sick! Can we land here?" My skin color was that shade that only someone with motion sickness can manage, you know the one, simultaneously white, green, gray and translucent. I slid down into my seat as far as I could. It is hard to lay down with a four point harness on, but I was determined. Guy is a professional. He kept the plane steady all the way to landing even though it was a relatively warm afternoon and there must have been thermal activity. In fact I recovered so much during the ten minute flight back to the aerodrome that I was almost able to take my head off my chest where it had fallen! He put the plane down gently. As I lay on the grass next to his trusty steed, waiting for the sky to stop spinning, he said, "Give me a couple of minutes and we'll try again." I was unable to answer. My mother taught me not to talk with my mouth full!

Thirty Something…

For my thirtieth birthday, I tied a couple of my passions together. Champagne and aviation can, in fact, mix very nicely and totally legitimately with a small amount of planning. I hired a friend with a Navajo Chieftain (Vincent Zimmer) to take Claude and his companion, my brother and his other half, my girlfriend and me to Reims, the heart of the Champagne region of France. The plan was to have a champagne lunch at the very best restaurant in the region and then return to Belgium in the evening. It being an international flight (Belgium to France) a flight plan had been filed and we had sent a fax of notification to the customs people 24 hours in advance. The weather was bad and we were an hour or so late leaving. After an excellent flight we landed at Reims Champagne, a joint military, civilian airport. We were a little surprised to get no answer on the tower frequency after being cleared by Paris Approach Control for the ILS, but the landing was smooth and the fact that the tower didn't answer meant that we didn't have to explain why we continued for landing with the field somewhat below minimum visibility requirements! Within sixty seconds of touchdown, a van full of Gendarmes de l'Air were waiting outside our hatch. What could this be about? "Don't you know that the field is only open Monday to Friday?" In case we were unsure, he added, "Today is Sunday." We answered with astonished silence. After producing our copies of the faxed notification to customs, our flight plan (also filed 24 hours in advance including a copy to Reims) and our copy of the latest Jeppesen guide which stated that by giving 24 hours notice the airport would be open to non-commercial traffic, we were taken to the police station. We sat and waited an hour whilst the paperwork was photocopied, signed, stamped and dated in triplicate. We were treated pretty well though… When asked if we would like a drink of water or coffee, I said jokingly, "I didn't come all the way to Reims on my 30th Birthday to drink water or coffee!" Within a few seconds, a bottle of champagne was produced WITH THE GENDARMERIE'S OWN LABEL! The gendarmes and my guests all toasted my birthday - well after all it was lunch time in France! When we explained that we were late for the restaurant, a taxi was quickly found and the gendarme in charge called the restaurant to make quite certain that we would receive a warm welcome and not a closed door. We were told that we would not be allowed to depart until the following morning since the airport was technically closed until then. An overnight stay at the hotel attached to the restaurant was a popular inconvenience accepted by all with no hint of a struggle, it made the party even longer and added a fabulous dinner and breakfast to the trip. The following morning the gendarmes lined up to wave us goodbye. I include this photo and a copy of the label because without it who would believe the story.

Getting More Out Of Your Passengers...

Once you get a pilots certificate there is a lot of interest, by those people around you, in 'going for a little flight, just to see the house from the air.' You will learn very quickly to give a good safety briefing and not to miss out the location of the sickbags! My good friends Martyn and Laura came for a ride. Pilots like to use the euphemism 'the weather was not optimal.' Conditions were, however, safe and more than adequate for a local sightseeing flight so we elected to go. Laura climbed into the back and I told her about exits, seatbelts, extinguishers, all that good stuff. We went flying! After 30 minutes Laura went quiet but whenever I asked if she was alright, she replied with a crisp "Fine," in her rather broad Irish accent. When we got back on the ground, she more or less ran for the bathroom in order to be sick AGAIN! I did not know until later, but she had very carefully emptied out her handbag in the plane, used it to contain her 'sorrow' and done up the clasp afterwards to avoid the smell! So once again... in your passenger briefing don't forget the location and use of the sickbags! As an additional tip, pilots should remember that it is ALWAYS more uncomfortable in the back, and making good use of the rudder to keep the flight coordinated will give the passengers a much less stomach-churning ride.

I've Got A Flight Problem...

Flying isn't a hobby for me, it isn't an addiction either. It is much more than that! I think calling it 'my way of life' is probably appropriate. For most of the years I have been flying, I have done other work to support my habit. I have been working with computers professionally since I was sixteen years old. Even longer if you count the money I made by sending games into computing magazines. I managed to get some published from about the age of twelve onwards. When I finally started flying, I knew that I was in trouble. It very soon got to the stage that if I hadn't flown for a couple of weeks, I would start getting depressed. I worked for Credit Suisse First Boston in Zurich, Switzerland for about four and a half years. CSFB is one of the world's largest investment banks. My colleagues were well aware of my aviation aspirations, I regularly bored them with my tales of high adventure; that is in the altitude sense of the word 'high.' After weeks without flying, the level of my craving would get sufficiently strong as to become noticeable to my colleagues, manifesting itself as a short temper, day dreaming, talking even more than normal about flying, wistful glances at the sky and glaring at any aircraft that dared to over-fly. Then the jokes would start. Team members would beg me to go flying. Talk of a collection being taken to send me flying would come up whenever I raised my voice. I became more and more unsatisfied with my job. It became clearer and clearer to me that I needed to get out of the rat race and cure myself of my addiction... by indulging it. I left behind a job as Vice President of Electronic Trading Systems and a salary well into six digits, and started instructing, for free. I used to drive a Jaguar, now I walk. No comparison, poor but happy wins every time, well ok, rich and happy would be nice!

Which Way Is North?

Things can and do go wrong with aircraft. There can almost always be a happy and safe ending, providing the training that was so laboriously acquired is applied rigorously and methodically. I was flying back from Key West with my girlfriend, Joëlle. What you need to know about Joëlle is that, back then, she didn't like flying, actually hated it! The flight was on instruments, IFR direct from Key West to Naples across about a hundred miles of water. The navigation instruments in the cockpit, which were all operating correctly before takeoff, were a Horizontal Situation Indicator (HSI), a fixed card Automatic Direction Finder (ADF) and a vertically mounted compass card. Most modern HSI's are 'slaved,' meaning that there is a remote compass system from which the HSI's orientation is set automatically. In my old friend N6298A, a tired Cessna 182, the HSI was unslaved meaning that it needed to be set and reset manually by cross-referencing with the compass. For some reason, soon after takeoff, the compass card decided to become a small motor. It spun about once or twice per second. Of course, (or maybe that should be 'off course'), this happened after a couple of vectors for traffic and once I was already in the clouds as you would expect. Joëlle noticed at the same time I did, "Is it supposed to do that?" As per the regulations, I reported my loss of the magnetic compass to air traffic control, Miami Center. I continued the flight until arrival in the Naples area by centering the HSI needle and keeping it there. Picking up the weather for Naples from the ATIS, I noticed that the clouds were almost down to the minimums required for the approach. Well of course they would be, wouldn't they?! Without the compass to reorient the HSI there is no safe way of determining the final approach course radial, the same is true for the ADF. I called Fort Myers Approach and reminded them of my problem. The controller from Fort Myers gave me a No Gyro Approach into runway five at Naples, I could hear excited voices in the background over the radio. It was disconcerting to know that the man telling me to turn left or right in rate one or half rate one turns, and to descend to minimums, was some twenty three miles away. I followed instructions carefully and when I popped out of the clouds at 500ft the runway was directly in front of me. I gushed thanks to ATC, telling them they were doing a great job. I was surprised when the controller thanked me right back. Controllers have to log different types of approach to stay current just like us pilots. I had just helped someone stay current. The excited voices over the radio were the controllers arguing about who would get to give me the 'No Gyro Approach.' Joëlle didn't shut her eyes once during the flight and I think she even quite enjoyed it.

Are We Supposed To Be Glowing?

Come to think of it, that Key West route has been 'exciting' on more than one occasion. The first time that Ute and I flew down there, it was late one Summer evening. It had been stormy during the afternoon, but it had cleared almost completely. At this stage, Ute was still quite new to light aviation and hadn't had any flying lessons. Yet another IFR flight in the C182, N6298A. It got dark soon after takeoff and, being over water, I was on instruments the whole time. There is a popular myth in aviation known as Night VFR. Whoever tells you that you can fly on visual cues at night, don't believe them. If you don't feel safe and comfortable on your instruments, don't fly at night. Anyway, back to the story... ATC called and said that they were showing a 'few small cells' ahead of us and that if I liked they could suggest vectors around them. There was a high overcast making the intermittent rain and storm clouds impossible to see in the gloom and we had already gone through a few bumpy little cumulus clouds so I gladly accepted vectors. About forty miles from Key West, our latest vector made the world go black. Then the plane started to glow, St. Elmo's Fire. I hate it when that happens! Well actually I like it, but it does worry me slightly. Then the plane suddenly dropped from under us. We were kept in our seats by our harnesses, but I still managed to brush my head on the ceiling. Ute wasn't worried by what was going on until she heard, "Oh, shit," escape from my mouth. I was watching the altimeter wind down like in a cartoon. We lost about 800ft in a few seconds. The instruments showed me in a level flight

35

attitude with a good airspeed. I slowed to maneuvering speed and attempted to maintain the level attitude we were in, the altimeter leveled itself off about 900ft below our original 5000ft altitude. Few! No wait, its not over... Then the roller coaster for a few seconds, bucking up and down. Then a big flash. Then a few seconds more bouncing. Then, smooth air, a view of the sky, even a few stars. "I'd better call ATC and tell them they just vectored us through a CB... That's funny no answer, actually I did not hear the familiar click as I pressed the push-to-talk switch. I'll try the other radio. Still nothing. I wonder if we got hit by lightning? Better check the fuses. Oh. Oh dear. Oh. Better reset them then. Popped straight back out... I'll try that again. Hmmm... I wonder if the transponder is still working... Yeah, I see the interrogation light. I'll try another couple of times with the radio as I climb back to altitude before I set the transponder to 7600. Aha! Comm 1 is back on line, pity about Comm 2. HSI is still tracking. Hi Miami Center, yes we're back, yes we're ok, yes it was a bumpy ride, yes I think we got hit by a bolt. No, I wouldn't like to do it again. Do you have anything on scope between here and Key West? No? Well that is good news... Hello? There goes the radio again. Back up again... Can you coordinate with Key West Approach for our approach clearance? Thanks. Ok, cleared for the approach, no known traffic in the area of Key West International. Oh there it goes again… Key West Approach, N6298A, we are on the ground, thanks for your help." First of all Ute just sat there while I tied the plane down. No wind, no rain, clear view of the stars, beautiful evening. Then Ute got out and needed to be held. She felt kind of limp. Clammy is also a good description. Well, we can laugh about it now. Heading back the next day, all the radios were behaving perfectly (I had them checked in my absence but they were fine, I suppose it was a residual static charge that had upset them, or something got magnetized, who knows - you aren't far from the Bermuda triangle around there!) Remember kids, "No such thing as night VFR." I had not even seen the cloud we entered until we were in it, glowing green and heading towards a dent in the sea!

If At First You Don't Succeed…

Ok, guess where I am going… Yup, Key West again. The Cherokee Six I had booked was having its windows replaced, but fortunately, the Cherokee 180, N7975N was available. Off we go! This time, Ute is with me, in fact she is doing the flying in the left seat. I am in the right seat acting as 'advisor.' Ute's cousin, Douglas, who has never been up in a light aircraft apart from being ferried from Sarasota to Naples a couple of days earlier, is in the back. We got about fifteen miles out over the water when Ute saw the ammeter fall to zero charge. N7975N has electrical equipment all over the place! I call ATC and tell them we are turning back. We shut down both GPS's (one also serves as the Comm and Nav. 2 radios). I shut down the ventilation fan, Nav 1 radio, the ADF and after telling Douglas what we were doing, the intercom. After discussion, we left the transponder on. With all that lot on, I think that the battery would have lasted about 10 minutes, not even enough to get over dry land. ATC (Fort Myers Approach) coordinated with Naples and cleared us to land when we were still 12 miles out in case we lost radio. We landed in Naples, very uneventfully, and after just a short break, took yet another plane, a C172, to complete the flight as planned. Douglas was not in the least bit concerned. I think the phrase is, "Ignorance is bliss!"

Not Always A Smooth Ride…

When you think of the Bahamas, what do you see? If it's sun, sand, palm trees, tanned smiling faces and, of course, coconut and pineapple filled cocktails, you are in the majority and 99% right. My own experience had all that on Nassau the first day, ending with a night arrival in Freeport and an adventure finding a good hotel. As an aside, there aren't many places you can fly to at night, in the Bahamas, unless you have called ahead well in advance, which is why the destination was Freeport. The airport guard made some cash on the side by taking Ute and me to a hotel. After looking at the rooms, a taxi was ordered and we found something better! Over night the winds were high and I could see and hear the waves crashing on the beach from the balcony, the rain slapped at the palms outside the window and thrashed at the window pane itself. On awakening the following morning I was expecting a return to the Bahamian weather for which the area is famous, not the thickest fog I have ever seen in the North American region! The temperature was decidedly cool, about 13°C. Steady light rain gave way to a heavier downpour, which at least washed away some of the fog, but a low overcast remained. After a cool, clammy walk on the beach, with Ute, Freeport was loosing its charm by no fault of my companion! I picked up a weather brief which gave IFR conditions with very limited visibility all the way back to Fort Lauderdale, filed my flight plan and we headed for the airport. The Bahamians cleared their national debt by selling me some fuel and after preflighting the Cherokee Six, which stood in a 4 inch deep puddle, we were on our way. About a minute after takeoff everything went gray as we entered the overcast. I had filed for 8,000 ft. As I climbed, the ride got rougher and rougher. Reaching 6,000 ft I had trouble getting any climb performance or even maintaining altitude even though the Cherokee Six was lightly loaded. ATC gave me an altitude block, between 6,000 and 8,000, as I upgraded my turbulence call from light to moderate. A large jet up at 12,000 ft, almost directly above me, asked for another altitude, the pilots words were, "Any other altitude!" He was reporting moderate to severe turbulence! By this time, I was fighting hard, sweat pouring off me and only half way. Ute, on the other hand, who had a huge grin on her face, was enjoying every second of the ride, sometimes with her arms in the air, and making the appropriate roller coaster noises and gestures. It was before she started learning to fly, but she would probably do the same again now! The flight lasted one hour and six minutes instead of the expected forty-five due to maintaining the recommended turbulence penetration speed and trying to remain above 6,000 ft. I have flown five hour, non-stop, flights in light turbulence that took less out of me than the first half hour of that flight. About three miles out from Fort Lauderdale, the turbulence stopped abruptly and I popped out of the overcast at about 800 ft. It was the first time out of the cloud since soon after takeoff and it made me blink, almost as if the clouds needed clearing from my eyes. I landed, taxied in and when the lineman asked if I needed anything I said weakly, "Yeah, just a few minutes." I was so soaked with perspiration it must have looked like I'd had a little accident. Ute, who is now starting on instrument certification, looked me in the eye and said, "That was so cool! Can we do it again?" After some professional counseling we remained together!

Bjorn, Bird Slayer...

One of the joys of flying in Southwest Florida is the huge variety of beautiful and exotic wildlife to be seen. One of the hazards of flying in Southwest Florida is trying to miss the huge variety of beautiful and exotic wildlife! Bjorn, a young Swiss pilot in Naples building flight time, set off to Everglades City for a day out. He landed his Cessna 152 on the relatively short (2,400 ft is considered short in Florida!) and slightly scary runway of Everglades Airpark (X01.) Runway 15 is narrow, falls into the sea at both ends and has a line of fairly tall trees off the South side most of the way down the runway. Most of the time the trees act as a pretty effective windbreak, but a wind from the Southern sector can change them into a vicious rotor generator for unsuspecting pilots on short final, fortunately not the case on this particular day. AOPA's Airport Directory has the following to say, "Caution; boats cross waterways in front of runway approach; high density bird population in vicinity," but it is not specifically a bird problem at Everglade City, the birds have to share the runway with deer, foxes, turtles, alligators, crabs, snakes, lizards and I have heard that fish occasionally jump onto the runway, no doubt hoping to learn to fly. After eating, Bjorn got himself ready to leave. He lined up, applied full power, and accelerated down the runway. It was a hot, humid day, about 39°C and 90%. He was just past the midpoint of the runway and about to rotate when... "BANG!" The cockpit went red and smoke started coming from the engine compartment almost immediately. He aborted takeoff, hit the brakes hard and just managed to stop in the remaining runway, no mean feat! He got the plane off the runway and shutdown. The first we knew back in Naples was a telephone call from Bjorn who said with a quivering voice, "I hit a giant bird on the runway and I don't know if the plane is safe to fly." Richard, the owner of the flight school, John, an A&P mechanic, and I set off in a Cessna 172 and we were soon there to see the damage. Bjorn had hit a huge turkey-vulture! There was only one recognizable piece of the bird remaining so it had obviously passed through the propeller. On the center line of the runway was a 3 ft long, lonely looking wing, outstretched as though still trying to fly. The engine was covered in bird puree, feathers, blood and guts. The cockpit glass was misted with blood spray. We, somewhat uncharitably, suggested to Bjorn that he should take the wing and put it on his wall or have it mounted on the hood of his car. After cleaning off the engine and cockpit the C152 was good to fly again. The smoke had been nothing more than burning feathers and the Everglade City version of the Thanksgiving turkey roast! Bjorn, still shaken and with heart still pounding, decided to get a lift back to Naples in the C172 with me. We followed Richard and John back to Naples in my first ever formation flight. Bjorn was always known as 'Bird Slayer' from then on. More than a nickname, a title he had really earned. After all, if you are going to take on a bird, it is only sporting that it be the biggest thing you can find short of an ostrich!

Jeremy D. I. Vandersluis

Instructor - No, I'm Not Paranoid, They Really Are Trying To Kill Me...

Stopping Short...

My career as an instructor started with a bang! Quite literally in fact. Most checkrides while advancing through the aviation hierarchy may be taken with a D.E. or designated examiner. A D.E. is an examiner who is licensed, or designated, by the FAA to perform certain pilot certifications. The FAA has a more 'hands-on' approach when it comes to initial certification of instructors. Instructors are expected to represent the FAA when giving new pilots their wings, and for this reason, the FAA sends one of its own inspectors out to thoroughly test the skill level, knowledge level and indeed level of indoctrination of the prospective instructor. When preparing for the CFI check, other instructors 'encourage' and reinforce your confidence by telling tales of four or five hour long oral examinations before getting, (or often, not getting,) as far as the flight portion of the test. In order to dispel any myths about these marathon classroom sessions, I wish to state now that it is all true! The oral portion of my check lasted

44

about four hours and left me wrung out and feeling exhausted. Of course like most applicants, I was wrung out and exhausted before I started the check at 07:00 in the morning after a sleepless night. The oral went well. I had studied hard and knew the party line on even some of the more obscure political aspects of being an instructor. My examiner, far from being the ogre everyone had promised me, was a pleasant and friendly guy who I would be pleased to spend time with anytime. He complimented me on my knowledge and classroom style and shook my hand, congratulating me and saying that I had passed the oral part and that the flying would be easy by comparison. After a short break, to 'de' and 're' hydrate, it was out to our weapon of choice, a Piper Turbo Arrow IV. The check aircraft has to be high performance and complex, that means at least 200HP and with flaps, variable pitch prop and retractable undercarriage. The examiner and I had already convinced each other that the thing would fly, at least on paper, before leaving the classroom. All the paperwork was in order, my weight and balance calculation put the center of gravity for the vehicle somewhere near the middle of my stomach and I could certainly feel it in there with the butterflies. The preflight walk-around and briefings completed and all the examiners student-like questions about the plane answered, we settled into the cockpit. It was blisteringly hot, about 38°C, but I had already been soaked with sweat in the 20°C air-conditioned classroom, anyway that's Florida Summer for you. Off we went, me teaching from the right seat, the office of the fixed wing CFI, and him pretending to be a student in the left. All went well until the short field landing demonstration and I was contemplating telling him that he was clearly a gifted student. Short final, full flap, gear down and locked with the green light showing, brakes checked, perfect airspeed, negligible crosswind, aim-point just before the threshold of the runway to allow for the flare and give a touchdown on the numbers. Good contact with the ground right on the center line, flaps up for better braking action, progressive application of the brakes, a few hundred feet down the runway in a nice, controlled straight line and then... What the hell! The aircraft started to pull hard to the left. I fought it with the rudder, which also operates the nose-wheel steering, I tried to control the plane with any remaining aileron authority, and I released and reapplied the brakes several times in the hope of clearing any lockup. I could feel the examiners hands on the controls but he just seemed to be following what I was doing. I managed to keep the plane on the runway, just on the left hand edge. When we came to a complete halt, it was obvious that we were leaning slightly to the left. After calling the area traffic to advise them that the aircraft was immobilized on the runway, I looked across at the examiner accusingly. Before I could ask what he had done to sabotage me, he asked me whether I had been heavy on the brakes, or indeed if I had landed with the brakes on. I replied that I didn't think I had been excessive in my use of the brakes and that I was only covering them as we touched down. I shut down and we got out. The left tire had burst and appeared to be jammed between the wheel rim and the fork of the wheel strut. Walking back along the runway for clues, we could see no sign of a rubber trail before about four hundred and fifty feet after touchdown. We had maintained the center line until that point. After that there was a light trail of rubber leading up to a thicker trail and then the crippled aircraft. The aircraft was at a complete halt in under six hundred feet! Well it was a short field landing demonstration after all! The examiner seemed satisfied that I was not to blame and that it was 'just one of those things.' After a quick drink of water, (as an instructor I have discovered that merely imagining the water to be vodka has a similarly calming effect,) a tire change done in minutes by the excellent people at Marco Island (KMKY) and a brief phone call by the examiner to his supervisor, the examiner allowed the checkride to continue. I was almost in shock having just about resigned myself to a failure through no direct fault of my own, a discontinuation in FAA speak. The rest of the checkride went off without a hitch and I was soon shaking hands with the examiner once again and receiving my temporary airman's certificate. I think the examiner was impressed that I had kept the plane on the runway in the most difficult of circumstances, I have to say that I felt good about that too! As a footnote to CFI applicants, it is never a good idea to say, "Let's take this baby for a spin." You may be taken seriously either by the examiner or by the plane!

The Pilot Is Morally Obliged To Stay With The Aircraft...

Of course, later on when preparing for my MEI (Multi Engine Instructor) certification, things went much better. My friend Pete was helping me to prepare for my MEI. We had worked our way through all the tough stuff and then he asked me to demonstrate a short field landing in the Seminole. Easy! I came down final with good airspeed but started my flair way too high. I could see Pete grab onto the storm window on his side of the cockpit (the left) and start to lift himself out of his seat. We were probably about five or six feet above the runway when the wing decided it could not hold us up anymore. In Pete's bar-room version of the story, we were still fifty feet up. Bam! Another very short landing accomplished! Pete maintains that he was just easing the blow by lifting his butt of the seat. I am convinced that he was attempting to jump out of the storm window but that he forgot to remove his seatbelt and shoulder harness. If he had been faster, I am sure he'd have torn through the restraints and squeezed through the four inch square storm window, before I could get us down.

Pedal Faster...

When I was working towards my instructor certification, I had the privilege of flying with my girlfriend, Ute, who was preparing for her own private pilots certificate. The flight in question was performed with my instructor, Rex, as an observer in the back seat. Whilst it was I who first got Ute interested in aviation, I was not at that time an instructor. By no fault of her own Ute had passed through several instructors, surely a disadvantage when learning to fly, before I was finally qualified to tell her what to do! I commented a couple of times, as we were flying, that the ball of the turn coordinator was off center, trying to provoke some corrective action. When it became clear that none would be forthcoming without further encouragement, I suggested that using the rudder pedals to 'push the ball' back to the center was the way to go. Ute replied, "Oh no, I don't use the pedals..." I am not sure how long the silence in the cockpit lasted but Rex and I exchanged incredulous glances, shrugs, headshakes, and wordless mouthings. All of Ute's previous instructors had just handled the rudder for her. "Well you are going to use the pedals from now on!" Ute went on to get her certificate and uses her rudder wisely but she does tend to complain about having "sore rudder muscles" after long flights. It is not a requirement or part of the job description of a CFI to massage rudder muscles after a flight, but it is a perk of flying with your girlfriend.

Learning The Hard Way...

The FAA now encourages CFI's under instruction to fly with real students and a qualified instructor in the back seat. My own experiences, whilst confirming the value of the exercise, also lead to the remark that there can only be one CFI teaching a student at once. The student pilot should only get instruction from the student CFI (unless an emergency or dangerous situation arises.) This was brought home a couple of times when my girlfriend told me (maybe Rex too but I don't remember that) to shut up and let her fly. She landed the plane and gave us an ultimatum.

Licensed To Kill...

The best piece of advice that any new instructor could receive is to remember that every student is trying to kill them. Some students are relatively inept as killers, but you do on occasion find a student whose propensity for disaster is such that you wonder how they made it as far as the airport, let alone into the air....

Flying On Fumes...

I recently watched a 'difficult customer' taxi the airplane out to the runway, take off and return to the parking area after just a single circuit. I was particularly interested to know why since I had checked Mr. X out on the airplane, a brand new Cessna 172, only three weeks earlier. I described our friend, whom I shall call Mr. X, as a 'difficult customer' since he regularly upset people at the scheduling desk with impoliteness, called five times a day to see if airplanes are available but made no bookings, asked for planes to be fuelled and then did not turn up to fly, etc... He left the airplane, and his three passengers, on the flightline and stomped into the office shouting at the receptionist (a young girl) before he was even through the door. "I told you to have 815HA fuelled!" The girl at the desk had had 814HA fuelled and was quite sure that his request had been such. His defense was that she should have checked the schedule to see if he had given her the right tail number when he called. While this was going on in reception, I wandered outside to the flightline and visually checked the fuel in the two wing tanks. I could see none! The gauges also showed empty. On quizzing a passenger I found out that the engine had run rough during climb and on downwind and Mr. X had decided to land. Only whilst taxiing back to the parking area had he noticed the fuel gauges. I went back into the office and did some shouting of my own. I also removed my sign-off sheet, which is required for insurance, from the customer files and explained to Mr. X that he could no longer fly the airplane until he passed another checkout with an instructor and apologized to the girl behind the counter. He had risked his life, the three passengers lives, the lives of anyone in the near vicinity of the airport and of course the brand new Cessna 172, just because he was too lazy to get up on a step and look in the fuel tanks. He was lucky that day but I am sure that he doesn't see beyond his anger even now. Flying is all about good judgment, but a few common sense rules help. Runway behind you, fuel on the ground and altitude above you are three things of no use to a pilot.

How D'You Do That?

I maintain that CFI, the shortened form of Certified Flight Instructor, should be pronounced and written in full as "See If I." As in "'See If I' can still perform this maneuver as well as my student!" I have to admit that trying to teach some of the basic maneuvers sometimes requires a little practice on the part of the 'expert' instructor before being able to demonstrate to the level of performance that one is trying to illicit from the student. It can be a little embarrassing when a student who is trying to get to grips with steep turns or short field techniques asks for a demonstration and is shown something barely distinguishable from their own performance. A good friend of mine, and fellow instructor, when asked about his currency replied, "I have been flying intermediately." I think he meant intermittently but who can tell? As CFI's, we also have to maintain some little used skills, just to be ready for those curve-balls students throw. Another CFI friend of mine had recently mentioned that he was about due for some training. A few flights later, a student of his managed to spin them inadvertently. Be careful what you wish for…

Sad Truth…

One of the problems in aviation training is the fact that many young CFI's are simply 'paying their dues.' By that I mean that they are working up the requisite number of hours to join an airline. Working as a flight instructor is one of the quickest ways to accumulate flight time without racking up huge debts or being fraudulent in your logbook! The students of these instructors may find themselves abandoned overnight if the job offer that their CFI has been waiting for materializes. The instructors use the students as a simple resource, a means to an end. The next step for the 'orphaned' student is to find another instructor. The student, having been burned once, may well ask the career intentions of their next, prospective, instructor or might look for a 'career instructor' such as a flight school owner. Then the next major problem arises. Career instructors or instructors who are going to be around for a while don't teach the same way as the ones who are enroute to the airlines, in fact, no two instructors teach alike. The student has been used to one set of rules, procedures and practices and all of a sudden there's a whole other set! The student regresses before he or she begins, once again, to advance. In some extreme cases students get passed from one instructor to another so many times that they are confused, lose interest or become disillusioned with the whole exercise. I made friends with a private student when I was working on my instrument and commercial tickets. He was and is a busy man and his flights were hard for him to schedule. In the last three years I got through a bunch of ratings as an instructor and as a commercial pilot. So far, he has flown with five different instructors, most recently me being one of them. He is still working on his private, I feel through no fault of his own. He really has been done a disservice by the system, held back by his instructors rather than pushed forward. It is a sad day when CFI's become Casual Flight Instructors or in some cases, Certified Flight Irritators, instead of Committed Flight Instructors and Completely Fine Individuals! As a footnote, I am pleased to say that the student in question finally got his private, and is now working on his instruments.

Jeremy D. I. Vandersluis

Oops!

Just because I am an instructor doesn't mean I don't screw up... There are dangers in aviation that are easy to dismiss until they are faced in the first person. It is often said that aviation accidents don't occur as a result of a single problem or circumstance but are the culmination of a number of bad decisions and compounding of problems. It is true to say that most incidents start before the aircraft has even left the ground. One afternoon, having already flown a few hours during a day in which my wheels first lifted of the runway at seven in the morning, I was asked to pick up a couple of stranded ferry pilots at just past midnight from Tampa International. Just a short hop really, a little over an hour away. Doing a favor for the flight school owner, always a good move, and picking up free hours at the same time was enough to make me accept the mission, the first mistake. I preflighted the plane I intended to use for the trip in the daylight, noting that it did not have an operative landing or taxi light. It may surprise some people to know that, unless the airplane is for hire, it is not a requirement to have a landing light for night flight. I decided that I knew my home airport, Naples, sufficiently well and that the airport lighting would be enough for me and elected to go anyway, bad judgment and more than a little cocky! I went home and got an hour of sleep, not really enough and certainly another mistake, but better than nothing. The IFR flight itself from Naples to Tampa was routine and the evening was relatively clear. I arrived on time at Tampa only to find that the ferry pilots' flight in still wasn't on the ground. Another hour of waiting, was used to explore the FBO and drink coffee rather than sleeping, still another mistake. The passengers finally showed up and, rather than electing to sleep for a while longer, I said, "Let's go." 'Get-home-itus' is a well known ailment amongst pilots and even experienced pilots suffer from it, yet another bad move. Once again, the flight itself was uneventful and the landing on runway 32 was good enough for the passengers to sleep through. I taxied off at mid-point of the runway, a messy junction between the two runways and a diagonal taxiway, this, it has been pointed out to me since by more experienced pilots, is not the best plan in the dark. It is better to roll all the way to the end of the runway and use a parallel taxiway with no ambiguity, mistake! Mentally, I had completed the flight and I am sure that I had ceased to concentrate to my fullest, big mistake, a flight is not over until the engine is shut down and the airplane is secured, relaxing at the controls of a moving aircraft is Russian

Roulette. I taxied down the diagonal taxiway (Golf) to an even more complicated taxiway junction (two parallels, Alpha and Bravo, and the diagonal, Golf, all cross) and made a left onto what I thought was the parallel taxiway (Alpha), I was using the blue taxiway edge lighting to guide me since I could not see the taxiway over the nose of the plane and without the aid of landing/taxi light. Unfortunately, the blue taxiway lights shine the same way in all directions which can make it difficult to know which side of them you are on (NTSB please note.) Almost immediately the noise of the wheels on the concrete changed and I realized that I was on grass. The taxiway edge lights are spaced out along the edge approximately the same distance as the width of the taxiway and at the complicated junction of Alpha, Bravo and Golf, I had gone straight over continuing down Golf before turning onto the grass between two edge lights I thought were on opposite sides of Alpha as opposed to the same side of Golf. I should have stopped immediately, but I could see the parking area just in front of me and assumed I had just cut a corner. I rolled forward slowly to keep the ride over the grass smooth and after just a few feet the nose of the plane tipped down about a foot. The prop stopped in soft sand with a slight jolt. The passengers woke up and asked if we were there yet! No injuries, no significant damage to the plane but more paperwork than you can begin to imagine. By the light of day the next morning, I went out to where the plane had come to rest and discovered a drainage ditch which I had never noticed during some years of flying from Naples. Whilst I was fortunate enough to come out of the incident with only my pride scratched, I learned several lessons;

- Complacency is a potential killer.
- Even if you are not yawning all the time, you may still be suffering from fatigue.
- One of the first things to go when you are tired or are in a low oxygen environment is your eyesight. You need even more oxygen to see well at night.
- Coffee is not a good replacement for sleep.
- On the ground, if in doubt stop.
- Even if you are in a hurry, it is better to sleep, takeoff when rested and arrive home late than takeoff and risk never arriving home.
- Aircraft lighting may not be mandatory for all flights but it is stupid not to give yourself all the advantages that you can.
- The airplane does not make a particularly good off road vehicle!

- Infamy spreads faster than fame… A few people at the airport still call me 'Ditch!'

Think Differently…

I flew with a student who had learning difficulties. He had about eighty hours when he came to me, usually more than enough to obtain private certification, but he had never made an unassisted landing. Previous instructors hadn't taken him seriously or considered him stupid and had assumed that, since he was unlikely to be capable of obtaining the required skills, flying was just a joy ride for him and learning or advancing further was not his goal. It is true that sometimes his reactions and behavior were out of the ordinary. During one of his first lessons, as we were approaching to land I said, "Nose up." There was no reaction so after a pause I repeated myself a little more assertively, "Nose up, nose up!" Still nothing happened and I gently made the adjustment to the plane's attitude myself. Looking across at the student I found him with his head tilted back looking at the ceiling of the cockpit. I was not specific enough when I said, "Nose up." I should have said, "Raise the nose of the plane a little," or "Ease the yoke back a bit." It is easy to forget that not everybody thinks the way you do. I am pleased and proud to say that in a few hours I had him making unassisted circuits. I don't know whether he will ever get his private certificate but I am sure that he gets more out of flying now that he knows that he can land a plane on his own.

Right First Time...

At the other end of the scale, I had a young Dutch girl as a student, on holiday in Naples with her pilot brother and pilot father. I could have let solo after just four and a half hours! She had never handled a plane before but had often watched her brother and father at the controls. I had to tell her what to do just once, she would try out the new skill, and within a couple of repetitions make it her own. She was landing unassisted after about three hours and were it not for a little fear on the radio she could have soloed even then. The sad part was that she was only in Naples for two weeks and had limited time for flying. She was a dream student. I have come across 'old time pilots' who tell tales of soloing after a couple of hours of instruction and never having had another lesson. It scares me, but at the same time it must have been wonderful to have been there in those pioneering years. It is sad that there are not many of those old time pilots left flying or even alive. Each one is a legend and each one is a page in the history book.

Since I wrote the previous paragraph, I got a new student who was able to make unassisted circuits from takeoff to landing in just two and a half hours, including doing the radio himself... A natural. I actually got a lump in my throat and tears in my eyes!

Sex In The Cockpit...

Most people think they know the difference between men and women. I would like to add to the definitions. Men are the ones who think that to control something, anything, you have to maintain a vice like grip on it and manage every tiny detail. Women are the ones that can accept that a tool is designed to do a job and allow it to do that job for them. Obviously this isn't a treatise on sexual equality, inequality or sexual politics. The point I am trying to make is that when learning to control an aircraft, one of the most complicated tools and dangerous weapons that most people will ever handle, there is an innate difference in the approach of men and women. A man does not feel he is in charge unless he is forcing the plane to comply with his wishes. For a man, it is the act of making the plane do his bidding which gives him his belief that he has the right to call himself a pilot. All of this leads to a tendency to over-control and generally be rough on the controls, particularly as a student pilot. Many male student pilots feel that they are in competition with their instructors, an I'll show him/her kind of attitude. It is with experience that a man learns to relax his grip, his style and his attitude and only then does he (hopefully!) become a good pilot. Women, on the other hand, are usually more 'gentle' in their treatment of the controls, smoother in their movements and more prepared to channel the aircraft's power rather than subjugating it. There can be a tendency in female student pilots to be over-cautious but this is easier to deal with than its opposite. I expect that as the years progress, in this the second century of powered flight, the sexual stereotypes and conditioning will slowly break down more and more. Claude used to tell me that there is one thing that prevents a plane from flying right, the pilot! It was whilst flying with Keri, my first female instructor, that I finally understood what he meant. Keri flew very naturally, little or no effort evident in her control of the plane. It was from her that I learned to fly 'with two fingers.' I try to pass on the same understanding to my own students. I have said to a number of my male students, caress the controls as you would a

63

beautiful woman, corny I know, but I'll use anything that may work! One of my red-necked, white-knuckled, rodeo-style, male students, with a death-grip on the controls, replied that he was treating the plane just like he treats his women! I wonder if he gets many second dates! Come to that, I wonder if his ladyfriends ever survive the first date! There are still men who don't wish to get on a commercial flight with female crew. The sky is a better place if those few remaining idiots stay on the ground! Just in case you think that what I've written here about sexual equality in the cockpit is just an attempt at political correctness, let me defend my chauvinism. One of the reasons I like to see women in the pilot's seat is that, 'I like to SEE women in the pilot's seat!' What a turn on!

Lean, Mean, Flying Machine…

One often misunderstood control in the cockpit of most light aircraft is the mixture control. It allows the pilot to alter the fuel to air ratio going in to the engine to give the most efficient fuel burn. If the air is thin, as it would be at altitude or on a very warm day, it is necessary to decrease the amount of fuel being mixed with it. A rich mixture may cause fouling of the engine with unburned fuel and soot from partial combustion. Reducing the ratio of fuel to air is called 'leaning the mixture.' Different planes have different leaning procedures. In the cockpit of a Piper Cherokee Six I have the pleasure of flying occasionally, there is a placard above the mixture control. It says, "Lean On Taxi." I was checking out a guy in the Six and as we were taxiing out, he asked if he should lean to the left or to the right. Sometimes you have to wonder if the people you fly with learned from the same pages you learned from... Or even the same books... Or even the same library.

Shaken Not Stirred...

Examiners are required by the FAA to administer certain forms of inhumane torture to prospective pilots and instructors. This is legitimized by calling it a 'checkride.' They do this in a variety of ways. Some stick to the letter of the guidelines, which are many and varied. Others feel free to interpret the same guidelines so as to 'develop a personal style.' Examiners are forbidden from teaching during checkrides. It's silly really, just when you have someone with a huge amount of experience in the cockpit and another perspective from that of your instructor, the FAA says they are not allowed to impart their skill. Some of the better examiners have found ways around the 'no teaching' requirement. My multi-engine examiner, I had the same guy at both commercial and instructor levels, has a neat trick to show candidates that in most light twins, a single engine go-around is a myth. He has you try it! Of course, since he would prefer to live through the experience, he has you use 3,000 feet as the ground or hard deck. In the hot, humid air of Florida, it can be quite a wakeup call! At the instructor level several patterns are flown on one engine but there was an interesting twist to my own checkride. The oral portion went very well but the flight test could have started better. The Piper Seminole I had hired for the occasion decided to fail the right magneto test on the right engine. I don't like to push my luck. I at least like to start each flight with both ignition systems operating. It failed so spectacularly that I wondered how I had managed to get the plane to fly at all earlier in the day. We taxied back in and after an hour in the hangar it came out with two new plugs on one cylinder, two plugs with significant corrections to their sparking gaps on another, and the rest of the plugs cleaned. Much better! This time we got off the ground. Later, when most of the flying was done, we returned to Naples for pattern work. I waited for my expected engine failure. I don't really know why it is called multi-engine training, after all you spend most of your multi-engine training hours flying around on only one! The engine failed and I did everything I was supposed to. My examiner gave me 'zero thrust' on the failed engine to simulate feathering the prop. I was still losing altitude rapidly. I wasn't expecting to climb, but at blue line speed, I should, at least, have been able to maintain altitude. Having rechecked my actions, I asked the examiner if I had missed something adding that if he didn't wish to add more power to the zero thrusted engine, I would have to land on the crosswind runway. My examiner, who was as surprised as I, gave me two inches more manifold pressure and that was sufficient to break the descent. The Seminole in which I did most of my training, and those to which the examiner was accustomed, had two bladed props, this one was three bladed. That extra blade was causing two extra inches worth of manifold to be required. Descending, when the airplane should have been maintaining altitude, convinced the slightly shaken examiner that it was probably a good time to get on the ground. I got my single engine circuit to landing in slightly too real circumstances! My examiner gave me two things; a temporary airman's certificate, and a commentary that would have made a sailor blush, about the three bladed Seminole.

Jeremy D. I. Vandersluis

GUMPS - Gear Undercarriage Mains Pneumatics Steerables...

It isn't always the newcomers that make the mistakes. Well actually, there are newcomers and newcomers. Through a bizarre twist of fate I once found myself checking out the guy I was working for. My boss was ex-military and, in addition to his several thousand hours as a single engine instructor, had a couple of thousand hours in fighter jets. In many twin engine jet fighters, the engines are in the fuselage as opposed to out on the wings. When the FAA grants a civilian pilot's certification on this basis, it is limited to center-line thrust. There aren't too many push-pull types out there, so a pilot with that restricted multi engine rating is more or less tied to Cessna Skymasters. Many military pilots don't even bother to get the civilian certification because of the limitations, which brings us back to me checking out my boss and getting him to signoff level for a civilian multi-engine commercial and multi-engine instructor license. However long one has been a pilot, getting into a new aircraft is the time to hit the books again. Granted, all (most) airplanes handle the same way. For an experienced pilot the way a given aircraft handles is unlikely to give any great surprises. BUT... you can guarantee that the manufacturers have done their best to ensure that the systems and the cockpit layout are as dissimilar to any other aircraft as is possible whilst still maintaining function. In the Aztec, the hydraulic pump is driven by the left engine. One unfortunate side effect is that, on loss of the left engine, you have to hand crank the gear down. Part of the fun of being a multi engine instructor (MEI) is surprising your student by suddenly causing (well ok, simulating) the failure of one of the engines. Most of the fun comes from watching the sweat break out on the forehead of the student, but fun can also be had by causing them to fly for extended periods on a single engine without the aid of rudder trim... Ah the joy of seeing the thigh trembling with the effort, the bliss of seeing the student hobble from the aircraft at the end of the session. In fact, it takes you back to the day your own instructor took pleasure in doing the same thing to you! Anyway, one day in the pattern, I failed the left engine on Hans. He hit the gear lever on final approach and waited... The GUMPS checks (Gas, Undercarriage, Mixture, Props and Seatbelts) suddenly became Gear, Undercarriage, Mains, Pneumatics and Steerables as after a few seconds he realized that no green lights were showing. He commented, "Ah, you got me," and started playing with the navigation light control assuming that I had been tampering. Piper products generally have gear extension lights which dim when the navigation lights are on. We were at four hundred feet by the time he figured out what was really going on and reached for the manual gear extension checklist. It takes a while to hand crank the gear in the Aztec. I gave him the engine back and had him do a go-around. He was a little shaken by the experience. You can be the best pilot in the world, but if you don't know the quirks of the plane that you are belted in to, it may be the last outfit you ever wear! Hans will not forget that the left engine is the "gear-engine." He learned something. I learned something about the way people learn. Hans is one of the best instructors I know, maybe the best. He also taught me something about flight fundamentals that day. He said, "If you want an airplane to go up, pull back on the yoke. If you want it to go down, pull back more!"

All The Right Gear...

A while ago I had to make an emergency gear extension. I was flying with a friend in his Arrow. A quick jaunt across Florida, me helping him out on the radio in the busy Miami class bravo, him doing the flying. In the back, another friend was along for the ride. We got back to Naples without a hitch but on downwind, when he tried to lower the gear... nothing. He tried cycling it a couple of times but still nothing. No 'gear in transit' light, no buffeting as the gear enters the airflow and no reassuring "thunk," as the gear locks. Being an instructor has disadvantages… when things go wrong, the person in the left seat automatically assumes that the instructor in the right seat can sort it out. My friend turned to me and said, "Your airplane." To which I replied, "I have it." I called the tower for a visual confirmation of the gear state having checked the circuit breakers. After a flyby they said it was all still up. I headed out of the Naples control zone and a few miles to the East to try cycling the gear a few times. Completely dead. No indication that the hydraulic pump was drawing power showed on the ammeter. I put the plane into a shallow dive and tried extending the gear whilst pulling up, trying to use the "extra gravity" you feel at the bottom of the roller-coaster ride. Nothing new. The only thing left was a manual extension. Manual extension in an airplane where the gear is held up by the hydraulics is a relatively simple procedure. It does, however, make me nervous since it is a one-time thing if your hydraulic pump is inoperative. You don't crank it down, once you release the pressure the gear freefalls and hopefully locks into place. If you get a partial extension where not all three gear legs come down and lock there is a risk that the gear may collapse on landing or that you may cartwheel on the ground, both of which could ruin your day.

I asked my friend, now the copilot, to read out the manual (emergency) gear extension checklist. It took him a moment to calm himself and find it. Airspeed... below 100. Gear handle... select down. Depress the emergency extension switch whilst fishtailing the airplane (left rudder, right rudder, left rudder, right rudder... which reduces the air-loading on the nose gear as it extends forward). All of a sudden, three green lights; gear down and locked. Phew!!! If it had been absolutely necessary, I would have made a gear up landing to the grass strip at Naples. Maybe I'd have stopped the prop on short-final and attempted to rotate it to horizontal using the starter. In this way, damage can be reduced to little or none if the landing is good enough. Gear up landings are not really dangerous but they can mean expensive checks and repairs... Only partial extensions are scary. When I told my brother about the events sometime later, he asked if that was three greens and two browns! Strangely, I wasn't scared at all... I was just really angry at the thought of joining the gear up landing club. My friend was a bit shaken and very emotional about it all. I think he felt betrayed by his airplane, his baby. How dare it fail on him?!? Of course people's reactions vary, Tom, along for his first ride in light aviation said afterwards, "Oh... was there a problem?" They say there are two types of pilots, those who have landed with the gear up, and those who are going to... I guess I am still in the second group (*for now*).

What Goes Up Should Go Down...

When ferrying aircraft from one place to another, it is important to find out the quirks of the vehicle before leaving. I was acting as safety pilot for a trip from Chandler, Arizona to Naples, Florida. The second leg of the trip started with us picking up our IFR flight plan. We received our IFR release and takeoff clearance and set off. Nearing the end of the runway, we selected gear up and trimmed the for an extended climb to our planned and assigned altitude, nine thousand feet. The airplane seemed a little sluggish but nothing too unusual for a high altitude takeoff and climb. On leveling off for cruise, I was surprised to see the airspeed at a mere 115 knots. A Bonanza usually skips along at 140 to 150. I started looking for a culprit and finally realized that the gear light was still shining green... Gear down! It was bright in the cockpit and the light was hardly visible unless shaded by hand. A few attempts at cycling the gear yielded no joy. It was stuck down. Turning back to the airport we had just left would mean canceling our flight plan, but continuing would mean taking at least an hour longer enroute to our destination. No circuit breakers had popped so the failure was somewhat mysterious. We elected to attempt to raise the gear by hand (something it says in the Bonanza handbook should not be done.) The gear crank in a Bonanza is placed so that it is easy for the pilot to reach, just behind and in-between the front seats. Of course, when there are two people in the front, it is the job of the non-handling pilot to perform jobs like gear extension. Hard to reach for the co-pilot, the best option for extension from the right seat is either to climb over the seat into the back (made hard by the height of the seats) or to remove the headrest and lean over the seatback. Just so you can get a better image, our cockpit camera is now looking at the copilot's butt. It is sticking up over the seatback whilst he hangs inverted with his feet tucked under the front of the seat, to stop from toppling over. The crank is deployed and the book says 50 turns should move the gear from top to bottom (or in this case bottom to top.) We slowed the airplane to decrease the air-loading on the gear doors attached to the main gear. The first few cranks were easy but it got progressively harder, as much to do with the blood rushing to my head as the air pushing on the gear doors. After about 40 turns, the gear motor suddenly kicked in and raised the gear the rest of the way. A supreme effort to turn right way up left me out of breath in the thin air at 9000 feet. Magically, our bird now flew some 40 knots faster. We figured out later that our problem must have been some of the Arizona desert in the squat-switch, (A device that stops the gear from being retracted on the ground.) It is, of course the only time I have ever been inverted on IFR flight plan… That is my story and I am sticking to it.

The Best Bit…

It isn't all scary stories. Whilst teaching (or rather helping to teach, because there were quite a few instructors involved) my girlfriend to fly, I had a real revelation. She understands how I feel in the air. How? Because she is one of the lucky few that feels the same way. Not just proud but privileged, liberated, exhilarated, invigorated and a whole bunch of other '-ateds.' She comes down from a flight flushed with pleasure, pumped with adrenaline, almost religious or emotional in her joy and with the worlds biggest grin. It makes being an instructor totally worthwhile, rewarding and fun.

Jeremy D. I. Vandersluis

Professional Detachment...

One thing that the FAA say instructors should do which has always been a problem for me is, remaining detached. Sorry FAA! I have become friends with just about every student I have flown with more than twice. Every time the student flies with you, they are trusting you with their life. Every time you fly with a student you are trusting your life to them (of course the instructor should always be prepared and ready to save both lives.) In a situation where lives are at stake and trust must be given mutually, it is hardly surprising that a bond forms.

English Royalty – James The First...

I had a young student called James. Well actually, two young students called James, simultaneously. Let's cover them one at a time. James The First was something of a phenomenon. He arrived having never studied for the theory exam or having had a flight lesson. He had had some exposure to aviation, riding with his father in his plane, but no real flight experience. We went through everything just once! Little or no repetition was required. The radio calls were right from the second flight. The landings were right from the third flight. It took four days to solo. After a week we reached the first cross country. After a week and a half James The First passed his theory exam with a very disappointing 98%. After exactly 20 hours of dual and 20 hours of solo, the minimum allowed by the FAA, James The First was ready for his checkride. He took it and passed… easily, completing the course in just two and a half weeks of flying. The examiner's comments were for my ears only. He said to me, "James is an amazing pilot but don't tell him I said that because I don't want him getting big headed." By that stage I had already told James that he was flying to commercial standards. When his father flew-in, a few weeks later, James picked him up from Tampa International, an impressive feat from a low-time pilot. When James got his Private, as often happens to me, I had tears in my eyes. This time they were of mixed meaning. Joy and pride for his, and yes, my achievement, and I have to admit to some jealousy. I am sure that I will be able to learn a few tricks from James The First before very long. I'd like to put down his prowess to his youth, just twenty-one years old, but that would just make me feel ancient at thirty-four! He met a girl while he was over here and she assures me that he does everything quickly… Maybe we have to put it down to youth after all?!

English Royalty – James The Second...

James The Second was another young Englishman on the fast-track to a private pilot certificate. I have never had a student who was harder on himself than James. If he didn't perform a maneuver right first time, he would really beat himself up over it. Getting him to relax and take the pressure off himself was particularly hard and perhaps made even harder by an event that took place on our second flight together. We were flying a recently acquired Cessna 172. It had come from Embry Riddle making its maintenance record exemplary. After accepting the airplane, we had made just one change to it, the replacement of a single navigation/communication radio unit with a brand new one. The flight started normally and we went out to our practice area to work on basic aircraft control before flying to Marco airport for James The Second's first few turns around the pattern. If I remember correctly it was just our third circuit. On the middle of downwind I smelled a little smoke. Completely unconcerned, I dismissed it as coming from the nearby farmed fields or the Everglades. There is always something burning near Marco. About the same time that James mentioned he could smell smoke the odor became

78

much stronger and obviously electrical. In fractions of a second the cockpit started to fill with smoke and I thought I could see a 'lick' of flame coming from the panel. I announced, "My airplane," and before putting my hands on the yoke, I opened the windows on both sides to vent the smoke. Once the smoke had cleared, I could see that the display on the number one radio, the new one, had gone dead. I turned off power to the radio which continued to smolder and turned the airplane towards the runway. On the way down I managed to turn off all of the other electrical equipment, unclip the fire extinguisher and remind James of how to unbuckle the seatbelt and unlatch the doors. I told him not to wait for me but to set off and run a safe distance back from the plane as soon as we were stationary. I landed long, deliberately, so as to be close to the ramp area. The landing was good and I had the mixture pulled and the fuel turned off as we coasted on to the ramp. James was out and running as soon as I hit the brakes. I followed just a second later. Once we were about fifty feet from the airplane, we stopped. I immediately started shaking and we both started laughing nervously. Not the most appropriate reaction, but with adrenaline pumping and the relief flooding through, I didn't have any choice in the matter. After calming down, I debriefed James on what had occurred and the actions I had taken. I would rather have an engine fire in flight, that is to say, on the other side of the firewall, than smoke in the cockpit. It really scared me. Rex came down to Marco with his tools and took out the offending radio, which smelled badly of smoke. He declared the airplane fit for flight and flew it back to Naples leaving me to take James back in the plane Rex had come down in. I was pleased and proud of James when he got right back behind the controls and flew back to Naples, but he was as shaken as I was and it was a small set back to our training. It says a lot about James that he was able to overcome it and got his private in about three and a half weeks. James went on to build one hundred and fifty hours of flight time in less than three months. I am pleased to say that one of his favorite destinations was Sebring (KSEF.) Not for the motor racing. Mainly because they make bread pudding daily and it is just beyond description. Fly there and try it for yourself, at Sherriane's Runway Café... Mention me... It won't do you any good, but I might get my next portion free! Anyway, James The Second always brought me some back, and for that, I will be eternally grateful, albeit slightly heavier. Strangely enough, a lot of my students get sent there for solo cross countries. I know if they have correctly reached their assigned destination when they bring me back the bread pudding. Ok, ok… So it's exploitation, but an instructor's got to eat too, right?

It Is Not The Size Of The Certificate, It's What You Do With It…

James The First and my good friend Alan passed their checkrides within a few days of each other. The FAA Designated Examiner had set Alan the task of preparing a cross country flight from Naples to Bimini in the Bahamas. I have never seen the likes of the preparation that Alan went through. It was to exhaustive depth and a level of professionalism which I would not require from a commercial student. In short, he really invested in it and made me very proud. Alan mentioned to me that he had no intention of letting all his hard work go to waste and that he would certainly fly his planned route at some point. Just a couple of weeks after their checkrides, Alan and James decided to do it. My flight school requires a briefing with an instructor before allowing pilots to go to the Bahamas. During the so-called-briefing, Alan taught me a number of things about the procedures for flying there! Off they went together in a Cessna 172. They climbed nice and high and negotiated the worlds eighth busiest airspace, the Miami class bravo, somewhere over Fort Lauderdale. Just one and a half hours after takeoff they arrived uneventfully at Bimini, albeit with a strong crosswind. After a short but pleasant stay our adventurers set off again, returning by way of Fort Lauderdale in order to clear customs. They were asked by officials to produce their licenses and duly complied. "What are these?" Both showed their temporary pilot certificates and the officials, having never seen them before, let alone carried by international pilots, questioned their validity. They got by with a, "Don't let it happen again." Whilst Alan and James were trying to clear customs, some other 'corporate-type,' uniformed pilots passed through on their way back into the US and were surprised and interested to see the 'scruffy private pilots,' inbound with them. Alan and James received congratulations all around from professional pilots who would never have dreamed of going international with their level of experience. I know a good few professional pilots in Florida who have never ventured out of the state. Sometime later, we had a visit from an envoy of the Bahamian government and tourist office. The Bahamas is doing its best to attract tourism in the form of light aviation to the islands and is making it easier and easier to fly there. When I told the guy about 'my two bold boys,' he was so impressed by their courageous trip that he asked if he could use their story in his Bahamian tourism promotional lectures. I sat down to think about all this. When I was a newly minted private pilot, would I have attempted such a flight? I am not too sure I would have had the nerve for it. The examiner did Alan a huge service. A flight to the Bahamas is a realistic flight to want to make from South Florida. By setting the Bimini flight as Alan's cross country, the examiner demystified the whole international procedure. Of course, if any of my students don't want to face the trip alone, or require a safety pilot for a trip to the Bahamas... Oh, pick me! Pick me!

Before We Go...

Every Thursday night I give ground school classes to a small group of potential pilots. They are all preparing for their private pilot written test, all started flying around the same time and most are flying with me at least once per week. It has taken me a while to get all the names straight in my mind and to keep track of who has got how far with their flying. It is particularly hard to keep track of the who's who since I am currently flying with two Chris's, two Mark's and two Tony's. Mel turned up for a lesson, his wife was with him and seemed to be interested in videoing the preflight. I was just finishing with a previous student, signing a logbook and scheduling the next session and so gave Mel the dispatch box for the C172 we would be flying and told him to go check the plane out. In retrospect he and his wife seemed a little surprised at the level of trust which I bestowed on him. Some ten minutes later I joined them at the aircraft. He hadn't got too far with the preflight and his wife was still videoing his every move. I stood with her as she filmed in an attempt to keep out of the shot. My suggestions that she should ride along met with a little disbelief and an obvious nervousness. I tried to convince her of the safety of the ride by explaining that Mel was flying quite smoothly and that the experience would be nothing but fun. Her stare betrayed incredulity. "Has he been flying without telling me?" she asked. I changed the subject then went quiet and walked away, fearing that I had put my foot in it. I thought I ought to own up to my faux pas with Mel and told him about my little chat with his wife. "But this is my first lesson!" he explained. I turned beet red and tried to reassure him that I would not consider having a first time student preflight an airplane on their own. I had confused him with one of the two Mark's, actually the student I was due to fly with next, who had already flown four or five times. I am in good company, I have a dentist friend and a doctor friend both of whom admit to having treated the wrong ailment at one time or another.

What Doesn't Kill You Makes You Stronger...

Ah Mel... Whilst I am not sure I agree with his scale of measurement, it is hard to fault his logic. Mel's wife thinks I am a hero. Every time he returns home after a lesson he tells all. His wife hears how many times I have saved his life and draws the conclusion that I am his personal bodyguard. Mel has the most novel way of quantifying the quality of his lessons as he progresses. Accurate too. The FAA would not encourage it's dissemination, but just between you me and Mel... At the end of each flight Mel counts up the number of "Near Death Experiences," and if the total score is less than that of the last lesson, he has improved. Last time out we were down to just one 'N.D.E.' Great job Mel!

Jeremy D. I. Vandersluis

I Ain't Seen An Elephant Fly…

When most people think of taking to the air, they are thinking of flying with the birds, soaring with the eagles. They completely miss the importance of elephants. Any of my students can tell you how valuable the pachyderm can be. The electric flap control on the Cessna line (C152, C172, C182…) was obviously calibrated by someone with a sense of humour. If you hold the flap lever down and count 1-elephant, 2-elephants, 3-elephants, you will find that the flaps have moved by exactly 10°. This does not work with giraffes, gorillas, hippos or chimpanzees, just elephants… A couple of my students have confirmed this fact. Mel seems to be quite excited by this phenomenon. Until recently Mel had a little problem on the radio. It is fairly common for student pilots to be scared of saying something wrong on the airwaves. But Mel is over his radio anxieties now. Most of his radio calls are flawless, which is why I was surprised when he turned to final, keyed the push-to-talk mike switch and transmitted, "1-elephant, 2-elephants, Oh sh… Immokalee Traffic 1516V, Final Runway 09, Touch and Go, Immokalee." I am glad his flying has reached the stage where he can land without my help. I was laughing so hard I couldn't have done anything.

Whips And Guns...

The FAA also have some hard and fast rules about how to motivate students. I can tell you that no two students are motivated to perform well in the same way. The FAA states that bullying, threats, physical violence and offensive language are to be avoided. As a student pilot my own instructor and good friend, Claude, would regularly slap the back of my head when I was 'being bad.' The beautiful Keri, my instrument and commercial instructor would threaten to beat me with a wet noodle. She did become quite pink and tongue-tied on the first occasion that I replied with enthusiasm. I think I said something along the lines of it being an exciting prospect and to bring it on and what exactly would I have to do to be entitled to that particular service. Whilst I agree with the FAA that bad language does not give a good image of the instructor as a professional, even that can be a developmental tool. One of my students was an ex-paratrooper. The phrase, "He swears like a trooper," was probably written about him in the first place. After trying the soft-soap approach, the meek and mild, and a variety of others, I came to the conclusion that 'a firm hand' was needed. The drill sergeant approach paid off and he now has his private pilots certificate. He and I shouted and swore our way around the pattern and across the sky. Expletives for emphasis only, no insults aimed at each other except for locker room style jovial encouragement. It worked just fine. Just try to remember not to tell the tower what you really think of them!

Mad Dogs And Englishmen...

Sometimes you meet people you take an instant liking to. I find that it happens to me more with people in the piloting circle than in other arenas. I have to admit that even though I am an Englishman myself, I don't generally seek, or care for, the company of my compatriots. This made for a surprise when I met Sally. Sally is an English woman married to an American, Greg. Both are pilots and they own a Bonanza which they regularly fly the length of Florida to their holiday home. Sally came in to the office in need of a BFR (Biennial Flight Review) and a bit of a brush up. Unfortunately, the Bonanza has a 'throw over control yoke,' a single control which is pivoted between the left and right seats making it a little unsuitable for training. When she told me that she didn't really enjoy flying all that much but just did it to share it with Greg, she instantly became 'a project.' We elected to take a Piper Warrior for the refresher and BFR, and I promised myself that I was going to make it as much fun as possible. We chatted in the air and I kept the whole thing very casual. It turned out that the only time that Sally had really enjoyed flying had been when she had flown with one of my former instructors, Keri. After just a half an hour of flying Keri had asked her if she wanted to stop at a near by airport for a bathroom break. Sally had been so surprised that it was even thinkable to do that, that she had asked something along the lines of, "Is that allowed?" What Keri had done was to let her know that it was Sally's lesson, her flight and that she was in control of what she did with the time and with the plane. Sally and I had a great time and she gave me one of the nicest recommendations I have ever had on our customer feedback sheet. She said that my enthusiasm for aviation was obvious and infectious. I would like to try to 'infect' as many people as possible with that disease! Later Sally and I flew together in the Bonanza and I would like to think that I helped her to enjoy that a little more. When it was Greg's turn to BFR, he came to me and we flew together too. Greg has considerably more hours than Sally. One thing I have in common with Greg and Sally is that my partner also flies. It can be quite stressful having two pilots with different levels of experience in the cockpit. The pilot with fewer hours tends to feel self-conscious or inadequate and is often quite intimidated by the prospect of flying with their loved one looking on. I think that only time can cure that particular problem, but confidence in ones own ability may be better accumulated in the absence of one's partner. Anyway, flying with Sally and Greg helped to show me the reality of my own situation. It also helped to show me that not all of the Brits on the planet are bad!

And It's Not Just The Students…

Sometimes it is not just the people we fly with who are out to get us. If the airplane decides it is going to give you a work out, you had better be on your toes. Flying a Cessna 150 with a new student pilot from Germany gave me a recent reminder that if something can go wrong, it will… And if it can't possibly go wrong, it will too! Making the normal 45° entry to the right-hand traffic pattern at Marco Island Airport, Bettina was doing a great job of keeping us level and headed in the right direction. Pretty good for only the second lesson. Without any warning, the nose of the plane began to vibrate violently and the RPM's shown on the tachometer dropped by about half. "My Airplane…" Whilst trimming the airplane for best glide, my first thought was carburetor icing since I had had a little on the run-up checks. It is hard for many people to believe, but Florida mornings can be quite conducive to carb. icing with the high humidity, temperature around 20°C and a cold engine. I pulled the carburetor heat on slowly, thinking if it is carburetor ice, then the last thing I want is to melt the ice all in one go and have the engine stop all together as it swallows the resulting water. No change… A throttle reduction gave an immediate improvement in the vibration. No smoke, no sign of high oil temperature or low oil pressure and distance from the runway (just outside power off gliding range) were all factors that lead me to leave the engine at just a little more than idle power, a setting which gave no vibration. I called "Marco Traffic." Two other airplanes were already in the pattern. I informed them that I would make a left base entry for a downwind landing to runway 17 with a loss of engine power. I also added that it was not a drill since Marco is a prime training destination. The traffic on final acknowledged, saying they would make a go around, and the traffic about to turn base, called an extended downwind. I kept the plane high, passed over the threshold at 100 feet and slipped the plane down to the runway for a soft and uneventful landing, coasting it off the runway. On the way down I coached Bettina and she was opening her door as I flared. As soon as we were at a halt she was out of the plane and back a safe distance. I was close behind her with everything shutdown and the fuel off before we had stopped. My reaction, thirty seconds after, was a huge adrenaline rush and butterflies in my stomach. Bettina remained cool, calm and collected throughout the entire event. Her comment was one of the biggest compliments I have ever been paid, "I felt totally safe. I wasn't worried at all." A few minutes later, having given the airplane a chance to cool off, we investigated. Looking under the front of the plane, we could see that oil was dripping out. The local A&P mechanic pulled the prop through a few turns and confirmed that we had compression on only three of the four cylinders. An hour later, a colleague flew a C172 down to pick us up and Bettina flew the plane back to Naples under my instruction. Brave girl! Due to a mix up on the schedule that day, Rex, my boss, had nearly taken that airplane for a fairly lengthy cross-country flight. Assuming the failure had still occurred, and at about the same time into the flight, Rex would have been in the middle of nowhere, with ploughed fields at best, and woodlands or marshes at worst, to put down in. All-in-all, it was a good thing that Bettina and I had taken the airplane, but, given the choice, I prefer fighting with students over fighting with equipment. Four cylinders are better than three, two engines are better than one. Of course, if I have the option, I would like six or seven engines hanging on each wing, with each one capable of sustaining flight on its own, and with each engine firing on all eight cylinders!

Instrument Destructor...

Sometimes, when you get back from a flight with a student which has gone well, you congratulate and praise the student. If you are being honest with yourself, then you know that you are congratulating yourself on a good-job-well-done and trying to take as much of the credit as possible. The old, "Wow, I must be a wonderful instructor," syndrome. Sometimes, the self praise may be, at least in part, justified. Other times, perhaps not. Alan and I have been working hard on instrument approaches recently. Every time we fly, we review previously learned elements and add additional complexities. His basic attitude instrument flying is good and getting better, the ILS and VOR approaches now hold little mystery for him and holding is improving gradually. Time for NDB approaches. One of my own instructors is on record as saying that NDB approaches are the ones that separate the men from the boys. I prefer to say that NDB approaches separate the unprepared from their lives. I briefed Alan thoroughly in the magical ways of the NDB Runway 5 approach at Naples. We talked for a full hour and by the end we both agreed that we understood what I was saying. As we were preparing to leave the classroom, a NOTAM was being pinned up on the notice board. "Naples NDB out of service until further notice." A quick change of plans. Find the approach plate for Fort Myers International (RSW), NDB Runway 6 approach. And out to the airplane we went. Vectors to final at RSW and apart from over-correction a quite passable, coached NDB approach. Second time around, Alan flew an almost flawless approach that left me marveling at my prowess as an instrument instructor. Back to Naples for an excellent VOR 23 approach to round off a, really rather good, flight. I showered praise on Alan and made some comment along the lines of "You have the best teacher I know." Two days passed before I received a call from Alan. Alan admitted that his perfect NDB approach had been a total accident. At no point had he been sure of his position and he had just got very lucky! He told me that his desk was covered in scraps of paper on which he had tried to diagram the progress of the approach we had made. After the nth sheet of paper he realized that what I had briefed him on in the classroom had us intercepting the final approach course for Naples from the North, and that we had intercepted the approach course for RSW from the South. He had constantly been expecting turns in the opposite direction and was disoriented, (orientationally challenged for the politically correct,) from the start. Of course, all of this was a blow to my almost un-dentable ego as I was forced to admit that my teaching methods were obviously less than perfect. I suggested that next time he flies a perfect approach, he should just accept the praise whatever the reason, and should he wish to confess at a later stage, a Catholic priest might be more appropriate.

Checking Out...

When a pilot of any description shows up at the office wanting to fly as pilot in command (PIC,) a checkout with an instructor is required. Some of the checkouts offer surprises. Over the years I have checked out a number of instructors, both ex and current airline pilots, commercial pilots, many private pilots and even an FAA designated examiner. After some of the private pilot checkouts, I have stepped out of the airplane thinking that the pilot should be flying professionally. On the other hand, I have checked out airline pilots whose flying was so poor I doubt they would have met private pilot standards – to be fair, flying heavy metal requires a different skill-set from light aircraft. The real surprise comes when checking out an experienced instructor and finding that their basic skills are rusty or that their judgment is dubious. One older instructor I checked out gave me a few scares in a Katana DA-20. With one much younger instructor, the engine started running rough during the checkout. Rather than staying high or even climbing higher, he descended toward the airport over a heavily populated area and argued that the circuit should be flown normally... OK... can I get out here and walk the rest of the way.

The Zero G Game...

To some pilots or passengers, flight maneuvers can never be too intense. What would seem like torture to some people, is just fun for others. Pilots have already proven themselves to be at least a little adventurous just by the fact that they are pilots, but there is a breed of thrill-seekers apart from the rest of us for whom aviation is the ultimate roller coaster. When I identify one of these adrenaline junkies as one of my students, I have a few little games that they enjoy and that I will use as a treat to reward them for good progress, or sometimes just to keep it fun. I like all of my students to experience a fully-developed spin. I don't force any of them to try it, but I do encourage them to see the safety advantage that recovering from an actual spin offers. If you have seen something in a safe, controlled environment, facing it 'for real' is much less mysterious, certainly less scary and therefore easier to deal with. Often, I will wait until a student has passed the private checkride before 'taking them for a spin.' Many students do however, ask for spins 'by name.' Even though they are apprehensive, they wish to learn to be better and safer aviators by broadening their experience. It is not required by the FAA at the private or commercial level, but CFI's must receive a spin endorsement in preparation for their CFI flight test. Anyway, I would recommend spin training to anyone and everyone, some of the roller coaster freaks think it is the ultimate corkscrew. There is another game, which is a lot less educational, but does require a reasonable level of skill. It is a personal favorite. This one is definitely a treat for the more adventurous student and sometimes, a treat for me if I feel I have been particularly meritorious! First you take a packet of your favorite M&M's. Color is your choice, but I recommend something that stands out well against the carpet and interior of your airplane. (If an executive from the M&M's factory is reading this, my favorites are Dulce de Leche and Peanut Butter but only red or green!) At this point, I have to tell you that this just does not work as well with Skittles - probably the aerodynamics. Now climb to altitude, the higher the better. Line up your sweeties along the glare shield, (the overhanging shelf at the top of the instrument panel.) Apply carburetor heat and then pull the power back, gently. Ease the nose gradually lower and lower under the horizon and the M&M's will levitate... Zero G! If you manage to keep the M&M's floating, you are 'flying the parabola.' NASA spends many thousands on each test of this kind. I think they use a Jumbo for them! Anyway, now the really skillful part... Your M&M's are floating around in the cockpit, forming themselves into mini planetary systems. This is your chance to fulfill your destiny and become the god you always knew you were. Maneuver the plane so that the whole of the yellow, red or green galaxy enters the black hole, (that would be your mouth for you first time players.) When you have depleted the known universe, and deleted several major civilizations for your own selfish pleasure, the game is over. At about two to three thousand feet above the ground, start a very gentle recovery. A word of advice. Don't play for too long and let yourself be distracted from the downward progress of the altimeter! The NTSB accident report would make interesting reading... "Pilot was found still seated in the airplane, ten feet under the surface of the ground. He was surrounded by M&M's of all colors except red."

Something To Remember Me By...

The Zero G game is not for everyone. As I mentioned previously, I had a weak stomach for a long time before I developed my 'Air-legs.' When a friend asked me to teach a buddy of his intensively for his private, I took on the challenge. The student, who was only going to be in town for a few days, came to me with thirty hours of flight time and a couple of solo flights. Unfortunately, he had none of the required three hours of night flight, none of the required three hours of instrument flight and none of the required five hours solo cross country time. A lot of requirements to be met before the private pilot practical test. I knew that I would also have to cover the ground reference maneuvers, stalls and brush up the pattern work. For our first flight together, I decided I needed to give him a mock checkride to evaluate all aspects of his flying. He preflighted the Cessna 150 in the very hot, afternoon sun, and we crammed ourselves into the steaming cockpit. I am six feet tall and he had a good two to three inches on me! We left Naples, and once I was satisfied with his basic flying skills, I had him do a number of stalls. It would need a little work, but that was what we were trying to establish. After some ground reference maneuvers, we joined the pattern at Marco. The circuits were passable and we did about five of them in various configurations. After the second circuit, he was yawning... Alarm bells! Yawning is a sign of nausea. I asked if he was alright. "Fine, just tired." On the next circuit the yawning intensified and my inquiries met with the same response. The next time round the pattern, I could see him paling and a sweat started to break out on his forehead, I was about to ask again when... "Jeremy, I am feeling a little bit..." He grabbed at the window and managed to get it open. Just wide enough to vomit through. If I had had just a fraction of a second more notice, I could have side slipped the plane and put his side in the wind-shadow. Without that small adjustment, the wind blew half of his meal back along the side of the plane and the other half right back in the window. With the wind whipping around the cockpit, the atomized vomit misted all over us. I didn't wipe the back of my neck. I just didn't want to find out how much I had in my hair. "My airplane," I said dryly, trying to ignore the smell and avoid getting sick myself. I told him it was no big deal and tried to bring the plane down to the ground as smoothly as possible. He cleaned himself up and washed off the plane. After a few sips of water and a stroll around the ramp, he was fine once again. Back to normal color! We got back in to the airplane. I didn't ever tell him that the whole of the trip back to Naples, the odor had me closer to vomiting, than at any other time in my aviation career. He and I worked together for less than a week and we got everything finished without a repeat performance. He passed his checkride and duly left Naples. The next day, I kept smelling something strange. I happened to be wearing the same sneakers and after some investigation I found that the laces were all nice and crispy. Some students leave you with more than memories.

Jeremy D. I. Vandersluis

Other Instructors - Listen to this... this guy I fly with showed me what negative G means!

Who Needs Fuel Anyway?

The Ercoupe is a funny bird... It has twin rudders but no rudder pedals! The rudder is mechanically linked to the ailerons. It also has a peculiar fuel tank arrangement. The low-wing airplane has the two normal wing tanks but then has a small 'header tank' which feeds the engine by gravity. The 'header tank' is fed from the two wing tanks via a pump. All well and good most of the time. When a customer of ours bought himself an Ercoupe, he had Rex check him out in it. Sometime later, when a trip up to the vicinity of Lake Wales became necessary for the purposes of maintenance, Rex went along to assure the safety of the trip. The fuel pump needed replacing and, after completion of the work, the airplane was signed off for return to service. At run-up, Rex noticed that the fuel was reading a little low. The aircraft was duly taxied back in for further discussions with the mechanic. The airframe and plant mechanic (A&P) assured Rex and the owner that everything was normal. Rex still had some concerns and made a mental note to keep a watchful eye on the gauges. After just a short time enroute, the fuel showed very low and, suspecting a problem, a landing was made at the next airport. The fuel tanks were checked for leaks and topped-off and having found nothing unusual, our heroes took off once again. Twenty minutes later, the same deal. Low fuel showing on the gauge and another unplanned stop at an enroute airport. Topping the tanks required little fuel. All highly suspicious! The entire journey continued in such a fashion with some legs of the journey being more worrying than others. The stretches without airports in close proximity! On reaching Naples, the A&P who had done the work was called and he drove down to see to the problem. The fuel pump was installed backwards. It had been pumping fuel out of the header tank and into the wings all the time it was operating. The 'fix' was quickly performed and the airplane returned to service anew. It is so much easier to fly cross country when you have more than a couple of gallons of fuel to burn. Bringing fuel with you is the popularly recognized and standard procedure for flight in general aviation although the military sometimes pick it up in flight. Generally however, it is customary to transfer the fuel to the engines from the wings. Not the other way around!

Jeremy D. I. Vandersluis

That's Not What I Said...

Sometimes people just like to surprise you. Jim flew with a student friend of mine, Alan. Alan was sent out to the practice area to work on maneuvers. Some time later (quite a while actually) he returned wearing a smile and a new T-shirt with a skydiving motif. Easy to tell that the shirt was not from the nearby Marco airport for which he had a sign off. There is no skydiving in Marco. But, as the shirt made it clear, there is skydiving in Pahokee! Alan had made a cross country flight of about 70NM in each direction! The planning was fine, the execution was fine, just the authorization was missing. The thing is, once a student is out of sight, how do you know where the hell they are! I have considered tethering the plane with a ten mile long bungee, but I am worried that having reached the end of the tether, I would see a student's plane shoot past the home airport tail first.

The Language Barrier...

The first student my friend Pete sent out solo was German. This gave something of a language problem. Pete, like me, is based at Naples Airport. Most schools/instructors in the area like to leave the class delta airspace and train in the less congested, uncontrolled airspace of Marco Island or Immokalee. However, when the pattern is clear or sometimes for soloing students, we make use of the fine facilities Naples has to offer. It is always reassuring, for us instructors, to have a fire truck and the emergency medical helicopter crew within walking distance of a solo student! Pete told him to go around the pattern three times before returning for landing. Being used to doing his pattern work at Marco, that is where he went to do it! It can be quite tense being an instructor at times. They say that each cigarette a person smokes takes two minutes off their life. I think that soloing a student takes about a week off each time!

Missed Again...

Pete has also, like every other instructor I know, had some fun with the tower. The guys in Naples tower do a great job. Having made a few visits to the tower with students, I am still amazed that anyone manages to get as far as the runway without hitting another plane, let alone taking off and buzzing around the zone. Last time I was in the tower, I spent a puzzled minute wondering why the aircraft I could see in the distance wasn't getting any closer. All of a sudden the dot I was watching took off, buzzed around inside the tower, and then landed on the radar screen. Just as well I don't work in the tower really! Back to Pete. He was taking a personal flight out of Naples. The active runway was 14. As he taxied out to the runway he overheard ground control clearing a light jet for taxi to runway 5. The jet needed the additional runway length offered by 5. After completing his run-up and changing to tower frequency, he heard the controller clear the same jet to taxi into position and hold. A few moments later, he too received the position and hold clearance. He heard the tower clear the jet for takeoff, but did not see it go. Probably busy reviewing his checklist or filing his nails. The tower gave Pete his takeoff clearance a couple of seconds later. Prior to accepting the clearance, he wanted to verify the jet had departed. The tower replied in the affirmative. Pete accepted the takeoff clearance and added that he must have missed him (meaning missed seeing him.) Tower answered that that was the general intention! When the tower arranges it so that we pilots all manage to 'miss each other,' they have won. When the tower doesn't manage that, it is the pilot who loses. Fortunately the FAA has cleverly come up with a plan to let at least some aircraft to get to there final destinations unhindered. There is so much paperwork involved in any collision, that it is sufficient incentive for the tower to keep us all apart!

Game Over...

My colleague Markus recently had a student, Bradley, who fairly rapidly obtained his private certificate. After about his sixth lesson with Bradley, Markus came back looking a little worried and concerned. I asked why. This one liner really gives an idea of what we are up against when presented with a new private pilot candidate. "He compares every exercise to elements in video games he has played... In video games you get three lives," he replied. I sympathized. Students often say stuff which give instructors sleepless nights. Bradley got his certificate, turned out to be a pretty good pilot and, as far as I know, still hasn't used any of his three lives.

A Roll Of The Dice...

Claude, my first instructor, was working with a private student in a Piper Cub. In the Cub, the seating is tandem, that is one behind the other. Claude's student had about fifteen hours, the stage when most new pilots have just about perfected landing techniques. The guy in question landed acceptably about a third of the time, beautifully about a third of the time and the remaining third of the time Claude described as "near crashes." One day, on final approach, Claude swiveled around (no mean feat in a Cub) to find out what was going on. What Claude saw must have been 'a little disconcerting.' His student had his eyes shut and his chin raised as if in a trance. Claude inquired just what the hell he might be doing and got the reply, "I can feel it! I can feel it!" I have heard flying the Cub described as 'seat of the pants flying' but I don't think it is meant to be taken literally, neither have I have seen 'using the force' suggested in any of the training literature as a legitimate technique.

Rollup, Rollup...

I witnessed this one... In Belgium, they think the same way as I do about night VFR. However they go that little step further and make VFR night flight, other than in the vicinity of an airport, prohibited. Perhaps a little draconian, but that is the way of the Belgium aviation bureaucracy. Claude was out in the pattern with another old friend, Guy. Guy, who spends most of his daylight hours flying aerobatics, needed to go out and re-qualify for night passenger carrying privileges. They were out for about half an hour. I was watching from the window of the bar as they came down final for their full-stop landing. I could barely believe it as I watched the red position indicator move from the right (its on the left wing but I was watching from the front) to the vertical, then to the left, then to below, and finally, back to where it started. A full barrel roll at night on final! I make no comment other than, "Don't try this at home, kids!"

Barnstorming Requires A License...

Elsewhere in this text, I mentioned that there are some notable exceptions to the earliest solo flights being simple circuits of the airport. The first exception I'd like to recount was told to me by my old friend Claude. He used the story allegorically to illustrate why a student pilot should never be told in advance the exact date or time that they will be allowed to make their first solo. He told a student of his that he would solo the next time out. The guy in question called all his friends and had them assemble to witness the event. The twist to the tale is that he had them meet him at a, nearby, unfinished section of highway where he proceeded to take each of them in turn up with him for a quick ride. On finishing his stunt he calmly returned to his point of departure. The second exception to the rule may have something to do with instructional methods of yesteryear, or it could just be due to a negligent CFI, difficult to tell. This was related to me by a student of my own and backed up by his ancient logbook. In Florida it is not unusual to have ladies and gentlemen circa sixty years who flew thirty years earlier but didn't complete their private pilot certificate for whatever reason and return to aviation to win their wings much later. Dick is one such gentleman. Originally, when I prepared this text, Dick was about to take his flight test. When trying to determine if he already met the minimum hour requirements for obtaining the certificate, he told me had, and duly showed me in his battered old logbook, the 'long cross country flight' required by the regulations. I thus assumed he had had a reasonable level of cross country flight with an instructor. Recently I rechecked his logs and found that his long cross country had been his first cross county flight of any kind! To add insult to injury, not only had his instructor sent him on a solo cross country flight with no cross country experience, but it was only his second solo flight! The regulations now require a minimum of three hours of dual cross county for private pilots.

Fair Weather Pilots...

Dick passed his flight test and soon after, bought himself an Arrow. An Arrow is quite a handful for a low time pilot, but Dick rose to the occasion. About a year later, on the third of July, I was online when Dick's instant message window popped up on my screen. I asked him if he was planning on flying the next day, on the holiday. I launched into a whole speech on the dangers of flying on public holidays with fine weather. "You get a lot of those, 'Once in a blue moon pilots up there...' It can get really busy and, however good you might be, there is always someone out there looking to do something stupid." His reply was a little disconcerting. He messaged me that he was certainly thinking about going flying and continued, "Me and my son got caught in a tornado last Sunday and I did not think we were going to make it. Before I knew it, we were doing 206mph straight down." I asked him just what the hell he was thinking of, flying in conditions like those, and adding, "You must be nuts!" "It just dropped down from nowhere," said Dick in his defense. I told Dick that it doesn't really work that way. A supercell thunderstorm is kind of difficult to miss. "So... You didn't check the weather, huh? You know if you go and get yourself killed it will make me look bad! None of us want that do we?!? I think maybe you should read your meteorology book. Find out more about tornados." I have to admit that I was more than a little bit angry, but I didn't want to get too upset with Dick. I know he gets stubborn when confronted, a trait we share. Then Dick played his trump card. He completely diffused my anger with some of the most wanton flattery I have ever heard. "Thank God I had you for an instructor. I remembered everything you taught me. I cut the power, eased the nose up and we finally got it leveled out at 900ft from 3,500ft. It scared the s**t out me! Vne. on the Arrow is 210mph. I thought for sure the wings were going to come off when we leveled off. This all happened in about ten seconds." After almost managing to placate me with his 'your instruction saved me,' line, Dick added, "It was a great ride though!" Then I really knew he was nuts! Maybe he should just go flying on the sunny public holidays. At least that way, I will just have the normal, 'Oh-my-god,-I've-created-a-monster,' level of worry as opposed to the, 'Deep-into-the-heart-attack-endzone,' level of trauma!

Make Them Stop, Make Them Stop!

Some people just are not meant to fly! Another of my instructors, Jim, who is now an airline captain, related this story about a student of his who I have since had the 'pleasure' of flying with. I can categorically state that there has been no improvement in performance since she took him once around the traffic pattern WITH THE STALL WARNING INDICATOR AND HORN GOING ALL THE WAY. Before turning on to final approach she said "What is that noise? It's irritating me!" The student pilot in question had a considerable number of hours and was regressing faster than she was progressing. Jim had given up trying to get her to keep the nose of the plane below the horizon and was just there ready to save the day when necessary. If I remember rightly, he did not fly with her again much after that.

Help From My Friends...

When I first decided to circulate this book to a wider audience than just my friends and family, I started thinking that if I had had so much 'fun' with learning and teaching flight, others must have had similar experiences. I contacted the National Association Of Flight Instructors (NAFI,) which is a fantastic organization, and had them send out a plea for stories in their e-newsletter. I received some excellent replies...

A Fitful Start...

Rob Mixon, who has written a book of his own entitled, "The Art Of Broomstick Flying," sent me this horror story. It's one of those stories that makes you wonder if you would or could have handled the circumstances as well as Rob did. Rob was once, "Flight Instructor Of The Year," which means that not only is he a great teacher, but that he has had his share of failed assassination attempts.

While waiting on a student for a half hour after his appointment he finally arrived bragging about how he had been drinking and at a party most of the night. I told him to preflight the Cessna 150 we were flying and watched as he seemed sluggish with his walk and movements. We were at 3,000 feet and he was behind on everything he did. I asked him if he had ever done a spin and he said, "Yes." He also said that they did not bother him. I asked him to do a one turn spin to the left and he replied, "O.K." After executing a perfect one turn spin to the left, he stopped right on heading and recovered to straight and level flight. "Good job!" I said. He looked out of my window and gave a startled and gut wrenching scream... Looking out of the window myself and expecting at least a 747 to be blocking my view, I saw nothing but blue sky and detached puffy cumulus clouds. Turning back to the student he was locked on the controls, frothing at the mouth and rocking slowly back and forth pulling and pushing the yoke with him! Between his locked fingers, there was enough movement on the yoke to make shallow turns and he was holding the throttle in place. His feet were locked forward on the rudder pedals. Altitude was controlled using the mixture to 'kill' the engine in order to descend and mixture rich to maintain altitude. Clearing a land leveling machine on final approach and putting down full flaps so if the student pushed forward at an inappropriate time it would slow the impact, we landed at

New Tamiami Airport, now Kendall Tamiami Executive Airport, in Miami, Florida before it was opened. He pulled back just at the wheels touched down on the newly applied asphalt runway, it was then that I discovered his feet were also extended and the brakes were locked. We slid sideways and finally came to a stop. I was out of there! The construction foreman suggested I go back to the airplane and clear the student's throat from any obstructions. Initially, after his scream, I hit the student on the shoulder with my fist and found out that he was as rigid as concrete, but not being familiar with epilepsy, I had no idea what was going on. He had suffered a Grand Mal Seizure and was unconscious for that day and night and part of the next day. Another instructor had soloed him and he had made several solo flights. He was not aware that he had epilepsy. Should this have happened while he was solo, he would not have made it down safely... After this happened, students who had heard the story, would purposely scream while looking out of my window in flight. They would then look back quickly to watch the hairs standing up on my arms! (Of course they thought this was funny...)

You Never Can Tell...

I have had 'tough guys' turn up for a first flight, asking for loops and rolls, who have been reduced to a quivering wreck by light turbulence or the first steep turn, and I have had seemingly timid little old ladies asking me, "Could we go any faster?" and, "Can we roll the plane over my neighbor's house?"

I had a guy turn up in a flying suit, leather jacket with sheepskin collar, Raybans, the works. He felt sick after initial climb-out in totally smooth air and the whole flight lasted no more than five minutes! You just never can tell. Jim Leon, an ultralight and powered parachute instructor shared with me the following experiences.

Last summer was a record season for introducing people to the joy of flying and training in a powered parachute. One man came out to learn to fly this new aspect of aircraft and fell in love with the thrill of flying the powered parachute. He just had to have his wife try this great experience. Unfortunately, his wife was scared of heights and had never in her life been in any type of aircraft. The husband finally talked her into trying an introductory flight with me because he knew she would love it as much as he did. It wasn't just that, he needed her approval before becoming the owner of a new powered parachute – aviation is so addictive. I had a lot of talking to do to get her to relax and get her strapped into the seat. After some time of introducing her to the machine and the way it flies, we were finally able to get the engine started and take off. She didn't say much right away, but after a few minutes in the sky, she relaxed and when I asked her how she liked the time of ascending, descending, pitching right and left and even backing off to idle to simulate an engine out experience, the words that came out of her mouth really floored me. "Is this all that this powered parachute can do, can't we do some kind of roll or something?"

The next day a man came to the airfield from Chicago and wanted to see what all the talk was concerning the powered parachute. He wanted to go on an introductory flight. We went through the ground school, pre-flighted the aircraft, fastened our seat belts, and left the ground. He, like the woman the day before didn't say much and I started a climb to 500 - 600 feet AGL to show him the beauty of the area. At 600 feet he asked, "How high are we?" I told him and right away he said that the flight was over and that I had to take him back to the airfield right away. I'm thinking, OH NO, please not down the back of my neck and my brand new flight jacket. But as I was approaching final, he spoke again and asked, "How high are we now?" I told him that we are about 50 feet AGL. He informed me that if we could continue at that height he would like to carry on with the flight. We did some low level flying for a while and then came in for landing. I was sure he was not the type of person who would enjoy flying, but to my surprise, his next question was, "When can I come back and train to solo?"

Basic Instinct...

I received responses to my request for stories from far and wide. Noeru Kubo, a Japanese flight instructor sent me a very representative story of how most of us learn good judgment. It is said that good judgment comes from experience and that experience comes from bad judgment!

This happened to me when I flew for the Yokota Flight Training Center, a small FBO owned and operated by the services division of the US Air Force. My job was to instruct both cadets, in the pilot training program for the air force, and self-financing students. Yokota Air Base is located on the outskirts of Tokyo, still a heavily populated area. Buildings and houses surround the runway. The single runway on the base is oriented north-south, and is usable in both directions. The pattern altitude is the standard 1,000 feet AGL for piston traffic and 1,500 feet AGL for the fast boys. Runway length is over 14,000 feet long making it suitable for just about any military or civilian traffic. The high density of air traffic includes all sizes ranging from our Cessna 152's up to C-5 cargo planes. Navy F/A-18's arrive in formation from the near by Atsugi Naval Air Station almost every day, either for practice or meetings. On this particular hot summer day, I was in the traffic pattern practicing touch and goes with a cadet. We were using runway 36, left traffic, and my student was flying textbook circuits. Just as we were rolling down the runway for takeoff we heard the voice of a formation commander flying a group of 4 F/A-18's approaching Yokota. They requested a short approach which is slightly different in the Air Force. In these short approaches they would fly over the approach end of the runway at 2,500 feet, then make a hard left descending turn to join downwind for runway 36. After joining downwind they would make a normal pattern to base and final. By the time we caught first glimpse of the approaching formation, we were at mid field down wind. At an Air Force base, military traffic takes precedence, so we were initially expecting a right 360 for spacing. To our surprise the tower controller instructed us to continue on downwind and follow the F/A-18 formation to base. Since

Yokota is a controlled field we obeyed the instructions, although my concerns did not diminish. The F/A-18s did their initial approach, made their left descending turn and joined downwind further out than we were. At this point we were ahead of the formation but continued on downwind to since the F/A-18s was suppose to pass us on our right. The first aircraft from formation quickly caught up to us then passed us approximately abeam the runway numbers, with the three fighters trailing closely behind. At this point my thoughts were clear, this was cutting it too close, thus I told to student to reduce speed. I was going to request a clearance for a right 360 after the last of the formation aircraft had passed us. To my amazement the controller rejected out request and told us to continue downwind to follow the fourth F/A-18. This is where I made a mistake I plan on never duplicating, I obeyed, which at this point was not a rational one from my perspective. At this point we saw the leading aircraft turn base, followed by the second, then the third. I kept on watching the formation thinking, "If the lead aircraft is that close what is the fourth F/A-18 going to look like?" The fourth aircraft began it's turn on base while I approached the 45 degree angle to the runway end. To my right I could see the F/A-18, approximately 1,000 feet ahead of us, and for the first time I noticed how true collision avoidance books are. The fourth aircraft seemed to have no movement, relative to us, watching from the front Plexiglas window. As our aircraft, and the threatening F/A-18, approached in harmony my thoughts were clear. I was going to make the right 360 to avoid a collision whether the tower controller permits us or not. Taking into account time lapse our C-152 began it's turn, then finally pointed it's nose in a different direction approximately 500 feet horizontally short of the fourth F/A-18. My heart pounding three times as fast as it should have been, I could almost see the name tag on the fighter pilot's jump suit. Upon completion of this evasive maneuver, I followed the FAR's and radioed the tower to state my intentions, LAND! The moral to this story? Ever since I began training I remember one comment that my instructor would always keep on repeating, "In aviation never trust anybody!" It was my mistake to obey ATC instructions until such a point where a collision hazard existed. I am sure the tower controller had good intentions when they instructed us to follow the formation, but in this case I should have insisted on the right 360 for spacing. I've learned my lesson. From now on if my instincts tell me something is wrong with the picture, they are probably right.

Give Only Your Name, Rank And Serial Number...

Don Lindsay sent me a number of stories from his archives. Don is a contributor to the NAFI newsletter, Mentor. This one illustrates that sticking to the rules is good and sticking to ALL the rules is even better, provided that you know what the rules are in the first place. Don writes:

Years ago, I worked through a flying club and was asked by the president to do a BFR for one of the members. The member hadn't flown for about eighteen months and wanted to get current so that he could take three associates on a two hundred mile trip. Due to being somewhat rusty, I noted his extra diligence as he did a thorough preflight, then engine start and run up. After we were airborne and into the practice area, we had done a few maneuvers when he pointed to the tachometer which was indicating zero RPM. He dialed the emergency frequency on the com radio and reached for the microphone. I stopped him by grasping his wrist and asked his intentions. He intended to declare an emergency because the tachometer is a required instrument and our flight, therefore, was in violation of the FAR's. I explained to him that although the tachometer is a required instrument, we could finish our flight and have it repaired later. He still maintained that we should call in an emergency but conceded and we completed the flight as planned. His piloting skills were intact so I signed him off with a recommendation that he fly a few hours before the planned trip for confidence building which would be helpful in the event of an actual situation. I later called the president and explained the situation with the tachometer. He replied that he had been having trouble with a loose cable but that he would attend to it. Less than a week later, I received a call from the president asking me what had happened on the first flight and if I had recommend additional flying time before the trip. I told him the story and said that I had indeed made such a recommendation. It turns out that our student went up to practice as recommended and, while he was aloft, the tachometer quit again. This time he did declare an emergency. The personnel in the tower queried the validity of the emergency but acknowledged the same at the pilot's insistence. An FAA Safety Specialist met the airplane as it taxied in and questioned the pilot. The specialist explained that although the tachometer is indeed a required instrument, the second part of the regulation allows a flight to continue normally and repairs can then be made upon landing. The flight really wasn't in violation of the

FAR's and there really was no emergency. The specialist then asked to see the pilot's certificate which, as it turned out, the pilot had left on the night stand at home. "Well son, that's a violation and I'm going to have to write you up a citation." The pilot was so incensed that he later brought his pilot certificate to the GADO (at that time) and told the FAA to keep it. That was the end of his flying career.

Stop, You're Scaring Me...

Don also had a story to tell that I can really relate to. It doesn't happen very often, but there are some people who should just have nothing to do with aviation. When you come across them, it is hard to know how to handle them. Some of them are very committed to learning to fly. When you know that you may be destroying somebody's dream, how do you tell them that at best they are a danger to themselves and at worst, they are a danger to everyone else. Don has tact...

I had a student back in the early 80s who desperately wanted to learn to fly but who, unfortunately, was just one on those people for whom flying wasn't something that should be pursued. Few people fit into this category and many instructors are ill-prepared to terminate a student when it's obvious that the student just isn't going to make the grade. So I gave him my assessment of his skills as tactfully as could be done under the circumstances. His reply was that he wanted to go through the course for the fun of it, regardless of whether or not he achieved a license. Fine! As long as he knew where he stood, I felt better about providing instruction. Later in his training he indicated that he wanted to begin cross country training. I agreed and said we would begin training with the next meeting. He showed up ready and willing to go somewhere… With an Esso Road Map in hand.

A Lifetime Of Expectation…

Jeff Van West sent me four stories about his experiences. What I have realized from reading his and other instructor's stories is that we all face the same problems and challenges. Whilst each student is very different to every other, there are certainly patterns which an instructor with just a little experience begins to notice. The responsibility faced by an instructor is enormous. It isn't just stopping the students from killing themselves (or yourself!) Each student expects their dream to be realized. For many people, flying is the most exciting thing they will ever do, maybe the most challenging thing they will ever do. Attaining that kind of a goal is a reward in itself. The hard part is that if a goal is perceived as hard to reach, it may impose a level of stress on the student that could in itself be a barrier to its completion. If that goal is a lifetime's dream, the pressure that a student can place on his or herself is difficult to imagine. And throughout all of this, it is our job as instructors to make it all happen. What a responsibility! Jeff's first two stories, illustrate the up-side and the down-side of the duty we have to our students.

One of my first students was an architect in his early forties named Kevin. Kevin was getting close to solo, when a childhood friend of his, who was already a private pilot, called me. The friend wanted to congratulate Kevin right after he soloed and asked if I could call him before the big day. I got the friend's phone number and we agreed on a thumbs up signal to say the solo went as planned. Without the signal, the friend would pretend he just happened to be at the airport that day. Kevin's flying was progressing well. His biggest problem was his own inner critic. He demanded from himself a much steeper learning curve than he was capable of achieving and would constantly put himself down in the cockpit. No matter how much I reassured him, he still expected better from himself. Given this fragile self-confidence, I held off a bit on his solo to make sure it went smoothly. My hope was that a stellar solo experience would silence that inner doubter. When the day looked good, I secretly called Kevin's friend while Kevin dispatched the airplane. The solo went great and Kevin grinned like a little boy on the taxi back to parking. Dusk was settling in after we tied down but I could see Kevin's friend sitting at the picnic table in front of the FBO. I dropped back a step and gave the big thumbs up. Kevin looked shocked and very pleased to see his childhood pal stride forward with a huge smile and a hearty hug. The friend looked him in the eye and said, "Congratulations, buddy. You've wanted this for a long time." "Yeah," said Kevin with a long sigh, "Ever since that Aviation Merit Badge." Aviation Merit Badge? That would be from Boy Scouts, which for Kevin would have been 30 years ago. He had been waiting for this moment for 30 years. On every maneuver, every touch and go, 30 years worth of longing, anticipation, fear, and doubt had been riding along in the back seat of that 172. When he turned around the pattern 3 times that day, he not only left me watching from the ramp, he put to rest 30 years of, "Can I? Will I ever?" I now tell my CFI students that one of your biggest jobs has nothing to do with airspeeds or FAR's. Instead it has to do with the power of desire and fear. We all come to flying with our own inner voices. If you can find that voice and hear it out then your student can really learn to fly.

A Few Words Of Encouragement...

With just a few words or a small action in the cockpit we, the instructors, can make or break the confidence of our students. Sometimes a wrong word or deed will ruin just a circuit or a single flight. Unfortunately, it is also possible that a single action will cast a permanent shadow over the student, or even a qualified pilot's, aviation. Jeff describes something that I am sure every instructor has faced.

It was 7:30 on a clear summer evening when our office manager asked if I would take up an intro flight. I had just finished with my fourth student that day and had logged about six hours in the air and over ten on the clock. I was ready to go home. "He's already a pilot," she said, "He's just thinking about joining the club. And besides, everyone else is gone." The pilot and his wife had been living abroad for almost a year and were now moving to Seattle. Before leaving the country he had earned a private certificate and about 300 hours in Texas. "I'm very thorough about my flying," he said. He pointed out how he had 100 hours before he was willing to solo. He seemed very proud of this. I gave him a tour of the club and reviewed our policies and procedures as we dispatched an airplane. Regardless of the 100-hours to solo, he was very well trained. His preflight was thorough. He used his own abbreviated checklist. His radio communication was flawless. As we moved into position, I readied myself for the months of rust to show. It never did. The takeoff was perfect. He flew with ease and precision. Most of the flight would have passed a commercial checkride. Somewhere during that flight I relaxed and as we came back in to land I didn't get back on my guard. He flew a textbook pattern to a slightly high final. Our airspeed was fine but the rate of descent was a bit fast. When he reached for the throttle I expected him to add a bit of power to slow our descent for the last 50 feet to the ground. Instead, he cut the power and flared. He flared hard enough to balloon us up to 70 feet, set off the stall warning horn, and create noticeable stall buffet. My left hand hit the throttle as my right hand hit the yoke. I never said, "My airplane," and my face must have broadcast something between shock and panic. All that might have been excusable if I had gone around and given him back the controls to try again. Instead, I landed the airplane. He was visibly crushed. He mentioned several times how he had never had to have a landing taken away from him like that. I apologized. I told him it wasn't a big deal. I reminded him it had been a year since he flew and I praised him on the entire rest of the flight. I don't think he heard any of it. He didn't return any of my follow-up calls. Some of the other CFI's tried too, but none got a response. I learned early on that as a CFI I could empower my students with my praise and attention. That day I realized inattentiveness or implicit criticism, no matter how unintentional, could rob someone of his or her confidence just as easily. I hope that pilot found somewhere else to fly. It haunts me to think that after so much work to help people learn to fly, I might have caused someone to put down his logbook and walk away.

Nihongo Wa Wakarimasu – I Understand Japanese…

Jeff enjoys a challenge, just like I do. Once again, the biggest challenge gives the biggest reward. I know that getting a 'difficult' student through a certificate or rating gives me a bigger buzz than a gifted student who just cruises through the same rating. It was certainly my hardest won victory that had my heart bursting out of my chest with pride.

The student of whom I am most proud is a Japanese doctor named Yasushi. Yasushi was in the US for a year, on loan from the Japanese government to the Center for Disease Control, and was getting his instrument rating while he was here. I inherited him from another instructor who left to fly for a commuter. I was told, "The doctor still needs a lot of work." Yasushi's logbook told a different story. He had over 30 hours of hood and actual instrument time already, with the last two pages of his logbook showing nothing but approaches. Aside from some minor technique problems, he could fly IFR just fine. The real problem was in communication. His English was quite good, but he had trouble distinguishing numbers. Imagine having trouble with numbers and getting the clearance: "Cessna 52139, fly heading 250, climb and maintain 5000, contact center on 132.95." Full approach clearances were a disaster and trying to get ATIS while simultaneously listening to ATC was impossible. The problem was made worse by the fact that we could only meet after he finished work, which often meant we began the lesson at six-thirty at night and weren't done until after nine. At the end of the flight he was exhausted and dejected. Here was a successful doctor who traveled all over the world tracking outbreaks of exotic diseases and he was confusing his fives and nines. I needed some way to boost his confidence, both in himself and in his right to ask ATC for clarification. On a whim, I asked him after one lesson to teach me a phrase in Japanese. It only seemed fair that I learn a little Japanese since he was working so hard in English. The result was so shocking, it was like magic. Gone was the timid and subservient student. His voice, posture, and manner all changed. Now he was the teacher, the one in authority, and I was the student. Our first phrase was something I had stressed during the flight: "Jishin wo motte," - be confident! He wrote it out for me to memorize. To help with the communication problem, I had encouraged him to ask to leave the frequency to get ATIS information, even though we were working near, and in, Class B airspace. On our next flight I reminded him, "Jishin wo motte Yasushi," before he requested to leave the frequency to get ATIS. He laughed politely at what must have been a butchering accent on my part, but he was granted his request. At the end of each flight, he picked a new phrase. There was "Totemo tsukareta," meaning very tired, after 1.6 hours of solid night IMC ending with an ILS to 400 and 2. In contrast he volunteered, "Yoku yatta," or well done, as things really began to come together. I had learned nine phrases by the time of his checkride. After he passed, the DE took me aside and told me how Yasushi had gotten a bad vector from the controller. He began to turn, stopped, rolled back to his original heading and asked if that was really what the controller meant. The controller promptly apologized and gave the correct instruction. The DE had several Asian students herself and had rarely seen that confidence with ATC. Yoku yatta, Yasushi, Yoku yatta.

Stealing Home Base...

Every time I communicate with other pilots and instructors, I hear the same thing. Hard to define, but nevertheless there. Call it pilot's intuition, call it instinct, whichever way you look at it, it is more than just training. Before a flight, sometimes you just know that everything is going to go well. Other times, you just know that you should not leave the ground. If only we listened to our instincts more, after all they are there for a purpose. Instincts and intuition have kept mankind alive this long! Jeff, like all of us at some time, felt concern before the flight he recounts and decided to ignore those nagging doubts.

My morning student had cancelled, so I had a few free hours. Walking past the maintenance hanger, I saw Rob pre-flighting a 210 that had been in and out of our shop for weeks. "Where are you going?" I asked. "Maintenance flight," he said, "I need to go to 12,000 feet to checkout the turbocharger, so I was thinking of making a touch and go over in Port Angeles to get a bit of cross-country. Wanna come?" I hopped in and we fired up. As we taxied out I asked what the airplane was in maintenance for. "Annual," said Ron. Right then I got this strong feeling that I shouldn't be on that airplane, but the embarrassment of being afraid of a flight for no good reason kept me quiet. Ron tried to contact ground and got no response. I tried and got through, so we put "Pilot push-to-talk switch," on the squawk list and I handled the radios. The trip up to 12,000 feet was uneventful and, except for the radio calls, I paid very little attention to the flight. As a flight instructor you spend so much time watching students, traffic, and airspace that you rarely get to enjoy the ride. This was a rare treat. We left 12,000 feet in a descent for Port Angeles only 15 miles east the airport. To get down without a cylinder-warping power reduction, Ron put out the gear and made a series of very steep turns. In four minutes we were down to 2000' and set up for a 3 mile final. The ASOS reported wind at 5 knots straight down the runway but the smoke from a paper mill out of my window looked more like 15-20 knots at 1000'. Had I been paying more attention to the flight, I would have thought about wind shear, instead, I reported 2 mile final while studying the whitecaps out in the Strait of Juan de Fuca to our north. Ron said something that I didn't quite catch, so I turned my attention back inside the cockpit and asked him what he said. "We have no power," he said. At first I didn't understand. I had just made a radio call. In fact, the whole panel was still lit up. Then I realized we were descending much to steeply to make runway and it was awfully quiet. We switched tanks and hit the boost pump. Ron slowed us to best glide. With the wind, making the runway was impossible but just short of the airport, straight ahead, was a little league baseball diamond. With tall forest on both sides of the approach path, we had no other options. As we dropped below the level of the trees, I called for him to tighten his belt and pop open his door. No more than 30 seconds had passed since we lost power. Below the treetops, we lost our headwind and the 210 seemed to shoot forward. Now we were aimed to hit the 12' backstop fence about 9' in the air. Ron slipped hard and we touched down at second base. The pitcher's mound tore off the nose-wheel and clods of dirt came flying over the windshield. We slid over home plate and slammed into the dugout building and fence. The windshield shattered and dirt and debris flew into the cockpit. After we stopped, my first thought was that we hit a water tank. A moment later, I realized the waterfall in my lap was 44 gallons of Avgas pouring from a ruptured wing. I shouted "Ron! Go!" I saw his hand popping his seat belt so I knew he was conscious and I dove out the space where my door used to be. Since I had opened the door in the air, the impact force had swung it forward and ripped it half off the airplane. Ron and I met up on the other side of the backstop and each made sure the other was all right. Then we looked back at the 210. It lay crumpled, gasoline still pouring from the wing, and with all the lights and strobes still flashing. Two CFI's on board and we forgot to turn off the master switch! I later found out that Ron had switched fuel tanks just before the engine quit. He didn't think anything of it, since the checklist said to switch to fullest tank for landing. Ron had learned to fly in Cessnas and never thought much about fuel tanks. The 210 was the only plane he flew that did not have a 'both' setting. I had learned in Pipers and checked both tanks before take off (taxi on one, run up on the other) and never switched below 3000' AGL unless directly over a landing site. Had I been paying attention, I would have objected to the tank switch, on short final. The 210 had flown only 13 hours the previous year and had 3 pints of water drained from its fuel system. It had ground ran fine on both tanks, but our steep turns probably dislodged some remaining water. It was just chance it dislodged on the side we weren't using until final approach. My first instructor taught me to be a meticulous skeptic, even with checklists. Even though it says something in print, you still have a responsibility to think before you act. He also taught me to never stop flying the airplane. After my experience in the 210, I apply this rule even when I'm not technically flying. Now I watch the professionals almost as closely as I watch my students. Occasionally I see something I question and ask them about, but far more often, I see how well things can be done and I see a new level of proficiency to which I can aspire. Either way though, I usually learn something.

Examining One's Motives...

It is said that those that can, do, those that can't, teach, but where does that leave examiners on the scale of things? I was recently told by an examiner what had motivated him to be become one. He had been an active and successful instructor for a number of years but with no aspirations of progressing to the heady heights of examiner-ship. Then one day, he sent a well prepared student for a checkride and the student was given a fail by the Designated Examiner (DE.) On debriefing the student he found that, not only was the student in the dark as to why he had failed, but that the student felt he had deserved to pass. When the student had queried the decision of the examiner, he had been told, "If you don't like the way I examine, maybe you should become an examiner and see how you do." It is very unusual for a student to fail unjustly. Most of the examiners I have met would rather pass you than fail you. Indeed, most are so scrupulously fair that you could run their grandmother over with your truck on the way to the airport and you would still get your certificate if you met the required standards. In this particular case, the student went so far as to suggest to his instructor that the examiner might be short of cash and looking for repeat examination fees! The examiner's words to the student, "Become an examiner and see how you do," played on the mind of the instructor. Maybe not immediately realizable by the student, but by the instructor, a definite possibility. He made the appropriate requests of the FSDO, attended the appropriate courses, and has now joined the elite ranks of FAA Designated Examiners. I am sure that his appointment has done something to raise the already high standards of quality and fairness amongst DE's. I would hate to think it was easy to become an examiner. You should have to pay your dues in order to be allowed to inflict that much stress, suffering and anguish on certificate or rating candidates. As a footnote, the same DE told me that the FAA gave him a really hard time at his final interview. A whole day of good-cop-bad-cop. When he finally received word that he had been accepted, if it hadn't been for his love of aviation, he would have told them where to stick their certificate!

Teaching The Teachers...

A recent, chance meeting in my local aviation medical examiner's office brought me this story from Jessica Stearns. Jessica is a retired captain from Continental Airlines, and continues to fly as a CFI in her own J3-Cub. With a CFI candidate in a Tomahawk, Jessica was playing the student from hell. The usual huge variations in heading, altitude, pitch, bank and power, that a pre-solo student gives us, were being performed by Jessica with some flair. The CFI candidate protested that it wasn't realistic. Jessica was immediately able to answer that she had just given him a summary of the last four lessons she had taught! If a pre-solo student is given the opportunity to do something scary, they will. If you manage to survive the first few hours with a student, your chances of survival increase exponentially from that point! Come to that, if you manage to survive the first student, things are looking up for you as an instructor. I'd say that after the first two or three students, you've earned bragging rights, and after the first two or three years, you have earned the right to call new CFI's "Kiddo," and mess their hair up.

Use And Abuse Us...

CFI could also be taken as Compendium of Flight Information. We are not just teachers of students, but also their mentors, advisors, counselors and friends. Most students view their instructors as the ultimate authority on aviation. If they have any aviation related questions, the student will often bring them to their instructor, even once qualified. The questions or requests made of us vary enormously. We may be asked about cross country preparation for a student's big trip. We may be asked about something as trivial as interpreting a weather brief, or we may be asked about something as major as the purchase of a new airplane. If a purchased airplane is not local, often it is the instructor who is expected to ferry the airplane. Sometimes the instructor is even sent to view the plane for the student and make a decision or recommendation on their behalf. When a student's airplane is sick, the instructor's advice is sought and if a test flight is required after maintenance, it may be the instructor who will perform it. One of Jack's students received an unexpected windfall and decided to treat himself to a brand new Cessna 182. At the time, there was a long waiting list for new C182's as they had not been back in production for long. After about a year, the big day arrived and the shiny new C182 was delivered to Naples, flown down from Orlando. Jack arrived for the handover expecting to see smiles. Only furrowed brows were in evidence. On the way down from Orlando, there had been a bird strike. It left a nasty dent in the wing. The Salesman was asking, after the repairs, what kind of a discount would have to be offered for the sale to go ahead. The student looked to Jack. Jack thought about it for a while and asked if an airframe logbook entry would be made, since the airplane still wasn't officially out of Cessna's hands. The salesman didn't know, and had to call his office in Orlando. The Orlando office didn't know, and had to call Cessna in Kansas. The answer came back that there would have to be a logbook entry. History of an accident in the logbook would take at least ten percent off the value of the airplane before it was even delivered! Of course, on hearing the verdict, Jack recommended that the student wait for a new plane. The story goes on. After an eight month wait a new, unblemished C182 was delivered and accepted. When it came time for the fifty hour oil change and maintenance, the proud new owner made mention of the fact that it was using way to much oil. A ground run-up check used a quart of oil in fifteen minutes! During the maintenance, which of course should have been routine at fifty hours, two cylinders were found to be 'out of round and beyond limits,' and cracks were found in the firewall! Cessna replaced the airplane with a newer, 2001 model. The details of the deal are not public, but Jack's student ended up doing very well out of it. Sure, our students get a good deal out of us. We all like to help and guide them through the trials and tribulations of the aviation world. We would all, certainly do it for free, but it always nice when we receive a little 'payback.' One of my students offered me his plane for a honeymoon trip and a grateful friend let me take his Cardinal for a ride. Great! Call me greedy, but I am still waiting for one of my students to throw me the keys to his 747 saying, "Hey, anytime you need it, dude."

Jeremy D. I. Vandersluis

Afterword - If I Am Still Typing They've Failed...

Well, I managed to get through all of those flights without any one of those potential assassins I call students managing to kill me. Either I am over-cautious, extremely lucky or maybe my time is just not up. Whatever the reason, I am still here. When I think about my hardest, scariest flights, I often find myself smiling. When I think about my easiest, most routine flights, I often find myself smiling. I just have to be up in the air and that is all there is to it.

It is really hard to explain the feelings of freedom, joy and elation to a non-pilot. All I can say is that if you are one of those poor, unfortunate, earth-bound creatures, you can be cured. Get to your nearest airport and ask about lessons. Most places have special deals for trial lessons or first flights. If you are in the Naples area, come to see me. Let me introduce you to aviation. I love it and I hope you will too.

If you are one of those fortunate and privileged few that has proven themselves worthy of joining the exclusive club, that is to say, if you are already a pilot. You must know what I mean when I say that there is just nothing like it. I wish I had the expressive writing ability of Richard Bach and that I could share the feelings and emotions I feel in flight in the way he can. I have to hang around airports and other pilots, because these are the people with whom I share those feelings and emotions and to whom I need not even try to explain. How can you explain to a non-pilot that the tops of clouds make you cry? So anyway, if you are in the Naples area, on holiday or just on a 'flying visit,' come by and we will swap stories.

I wish you many safe and happy flights.

Jeremy D. I. Vandersluis, CFI/CFII/MEI

jdiv@compuserve.com

AOPA:01376218

NAFI:16536-W

Jeremy D. I. Vandersluis

About The Author

Jeremy Vandersluis gave up a successful career in computing and finance, with a salary well into six digits. When he learned to fly, he realized that nothing else could beat it. With no real intention of becoming an instructor, he passed the exams and found himself on the flight line with students of his own. He continues to survive repeated attempts on his life by those students.

Jeremy is an AOPA member and also belongs to the National Association of Flight Instructors. He is thirty-four years old and lives in Naples, Florida. He chose Naples because it is a great place to fly.